From the Hairdresser's Chair

True Stories
to Inspire
and Captivate.

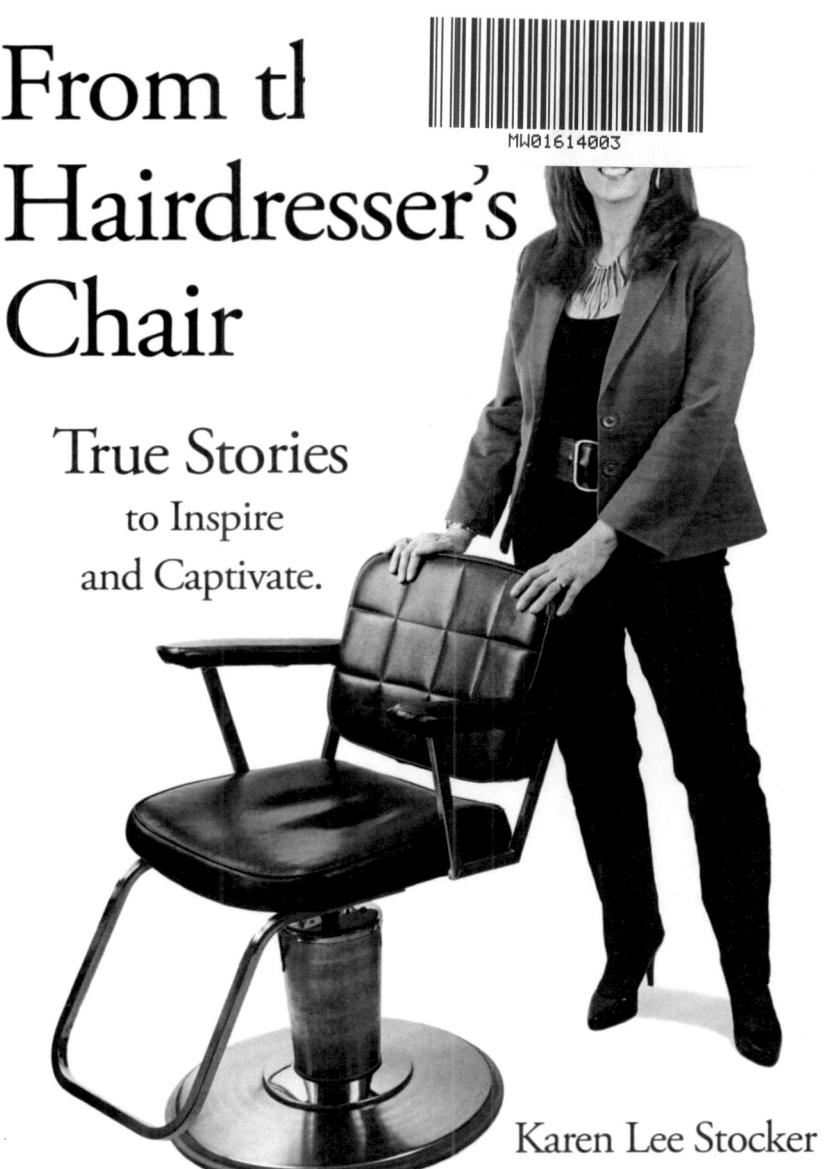

Karen Lee Stocker

From the Hairdresser's Chair

Printed in Canada 2015

ISBN 978-0-9947617-0-5

Publisher: KS Publishing
St. Catharines, Ontario, Canada

Cover Design: Canmore Printcraft,

Photography by Tracy Munson

www.FromTheHairdressersChair.com

DEDICATION

This book is dedicated to all the people who have ever shared their life stories in their hairdresser's chair.

TABLE OF CONTENTS

From the Hairdresser's Chair

ACKNOWLEDGMENTS

From the Hairdresser's Chair has taken more than four years to write, compile and edit. One of the greatest joys in creating this book has been working with the wonderful stories my clients have shared with me over 40 years. The idea for this book began in my chair. My client, Barb Smyth, said, "Karen, you should write a column about the stories you have heard in this chair." Great idea; so I did! The column was published in the Business Link Newspaper and in HWS Magazine. My heartfelt thanks to Barb for having initiated this book.

Thank you to my family, my husband Dave and children for all their love and support. My fellow Toastmasters at Honeymoon City Toastmasters, thank you for all your encouragement and evaluations.

Many Thanks:
My Chief Editor: Lou Anne Reddon
My Editors:
John Mowat: Co-author of *To Cry a Dry Tear*
Judy Suke: Co-author of *From the Stage to the Page*
Deborah Richards: M.A. Co-author *Ethical Dilemmas* and over 50 publications
Michelle Ashton: Teacher DSBN.

My Photographer: Tracy Munson for her excellence.

I am deeply grateful to my clients who graciously allowed me to print their stories and for the many caring hands that have touched this project.

INTRODUCTION

For as long as I can remember, I've always wanted to be a hairdresser. My mother told me I was cutting my dolls' hair when I was in Grade 2. As I was approaching Grade 10, my Dad tried to convince me I should work in a bank; he thought that would be a good career for me. I stuck to my dream and now I am reaching 41 years in this profession. I do have to say it is a young person's career. There are not too many people my age doing this job full time.

For years, I thought it was the craft I loved, until I realized - no! It was actually the magic that happened in the chair. Clients trusted me with many personal and career challenges. They felt my opinion was very important to decisions they were making.

The joy of this experience led me to public speaking. It comes from my chair, all the years of shifting people from their problems to a solution.

In 1985, I came across a book that was written by a psychologist. He couldn't understand why one of his patients, with whom he had been working for quite some time on a particular challenge, was suddenly ready to make a huge change. It was after she had talked to her hairdresser that she decided not to go through with it.

Amazed at the hairdresser's influence, the psychologist set off on a mission to interview

From the Hairdresser's Chair

hairdressers across the United States and Canada to understand the connection.

When I read this book, I knew right away what it was all about. Early in my career, I had learned that the technical part of hairdressing is only about 15% of the job. The remaining 85% is customer service.

Relationships are built very quickly in the chair and the trust is huge. Maybe it is because we go beyond that 18-inch comfort zone of ours and we touch the client. Or could it be the sharp tools we are using? Who knows? But the rapport is there with 99% of the clients.

Over the years, I'd heard so many stories that, when a client suggested I should write a column about them, I took up the challenge and created *From the Hairdresser's Chair*. It started as a newspaper and magazine column, but ultimately led to me writing this book.

My hairdressing clientele has dropped from serving 180 clients a month to about 80, so that I can dedicate my time to writing and speaking, to bring my passion for helping people to a whole new level.

I found that passion in helping others achieve their goals through delivering motivational seminars.

My clients always say they come to get their hair done, then the bonus is the therapy that happens in the chair! I not only help my clients, I also learn so much from them. They are unique; each one has come to my chair for a special reason. I look for the gift or lesson from each client's story or situation.

The stories you are about to enjoy cover all the key areas of life I often talk about in the chair: relationships, career, health, personal goals, fun and recreation and contribution. They range from challenges in these areas to lessons, feedback, learning, fulfillment, accomplishment, gratitude and appreciation.

Each story will touch you in some way and leave you with a different perspective on that area of life.

Enjoy the read!

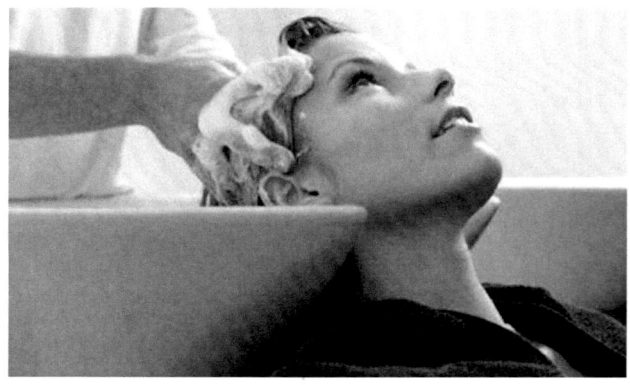

PART ONE

Nancy: The Best Role Model Anyone Could Ever Hope to Have

In 1976, when I was a very young hair salon owner, a woman called to ask if I carried a certain line of hair colour. I told her I did and she made an appointment right away. Turns out she couldn't find anyone, anywhere, who carried that particular line.

When Nancy arrived for her appointment, I found out she was from Buffalo, New York, but she and her family owned a summer home in Bertie Bay, near Fort Erie where my salon was located.

She was a lovely woman with a young family. Her son, Chad, was five and Mary Alice was thirteen. Nancy owned and operated a modelling school in Buffalo, the largest of its kind in America. She became a regular client every four weeks and really seemed to like what I could do with her hair. Soon her children were coming for haircuts, too.

One day, she said to me, "I want to groom my daughter with a professional look to her hair and prepare her for her future career." She was also grooming her son. Already, Chad was doing photo shoots for ad campaigns at the young age of eight.

He even went to a youth speech camp to help him with public speaking! Today, Chad is a nationally renowned public speaker and an executive director of his company.

From the Hairdresser's Chair

You could tell that Nancy liked to help polish and prepare everyone in her life, from the models she represented to her own children!

Every year, she would go to her Florida home and I would order her a five-month supply of her favourite hair colour to take along. She greatly appreciated that!

After a year of doing her hair, models from her agency started coming to my salon. They loved my work. I was still a pretty young hairdresser at the time and this really helped build my confidence.

One day, I happened to be watching the Buffalo news in the morning. They were going to be interviewing an international fashion expert. I decided to watch. Lo and behold doesn't my client Nancy come walking out to be interviewed? My jaw dropped and I said to myself, "Oh, my goodness! That's *my* client!"

I watched the interview and heard Nancy talk about travelling the globe with the models from her school. It was so exciting to think I had a celebrity in my chair! It really boosted my confidence.

Next time Nancy came in for her appointment, I mentioned the interview. She smiled quietly and simply said, "I like to keep some things quiet."

I respected her privacy, and I respected her. Therefore, I never, ever told anyone else in the salon.

I'd keep seeing her on television, as a fashion expert showing the latest top creations on the runway. She spent a lot of time in New York City.

During one hair appointment, she shared the amazing story of how she had once met and spent time with Princess Grace of Monaco. Nancy was a very assertive, yet sincere and earnest woman. She told me once that you would never know if you could get what you wanted unless you at least asked.

Nancy wrote a letter to Princess Grace, explaining that she was bringing a number of models from her agency to designer fashion shows and modelling agencies in Europe. She wondered if they might have a tour of the palace and meet Princess Grace. Incredibly, the response was yes!

Nancy, her daughter and her models toured the palace and met the princess.

She was an amazing marketer. She forged great relationships with the media. It was the 1980s; not at all like the social media of today. Nancy enjoyed relationships with radio announcers, television broadcasters and the chief editors of many newspapers and magazines. Nancy knew when to be loud and when to be quiet.

I enjoyed this private client of mine. I felt special having her in my chair and she trusted me. When the models from her agency came in for their appointments, they would all say she was a fantastic woman and an amazing mentor to them.

Thanks to Nancy's faith in me as a hairdresser, they trusted me too, and loved my work.

I remember one model in particular, Debbie, had had some highlights done before heading off to a fashion show in Paris. There, the hairdresser and photographer at the show had raved about her beautiful highlights! When she came home and shared this with me, I was thrilled to have received a compliment about my work from the Paris runway.

Over the years, I gradually learned more about Nancy's private life. She had a Master's degree in Christian Education. With this faith and compassion, she touched many young lives, as evidenced by her creation of programs for the deaf and blind at her modelling school. Her daughter, Mary Alice, created materials in Braille for these classes.

The expertise she developed through owning modelling schools allowed Nancy to help cancer patients who were disfigured by the disease. She designed courses that not only taught these special students how to do particular make-up applications to camouflage their scars and imperfections, but also helped them with their self-confidence.

A very giving woman, Nancy was president of the Zonta Club in Buffalo, and also founded Zonta Clubs in Fort Erie and Sarasota, Florida. Her kindness and generosity knew no borders.

I enjoyed having Nancy and *all* her girls as clients for many years. Eventually, she decided to sell her school and agency in Buffalo and work from Sarasota.

She and her daughter wrote a book together, called *Bridge the Gap*. It provided answers to the questions asked most often by parents and teens, from both generational viewpoints. The pair toured nationwide, giving speeches, workshops, TV, and radio interviews based on their book.

The last I ever heard from Nancy was that she had founded Volkert Meeting Planning, Inc. in Sarasota which Mary Alice eventually took over.

A few more years went by and a new client from Buffalo came to me. She knew Nancy from her church and told me that she had been very ill with cancer. Only a few months later, she arrived with news that Nancy had passed away and she brought in the obituary for me.

It's now three decades later and here I am, writing about this extraordinary woman who graced my chair. I decided to Google her daughter. Isn't it amazing what you can find on the internet?

From the Hairdresser's Chair

I found Mary Alice in Florida! She remembered me and we shared many stories from the past about her mother.

Nancy's husband, Chuck, her daughter and son, Mary Alice and Chad, said they would be honoured to have me write about her.

Having a client like Nancy gave me the confidence I needed to move forward in my career as a hairdresser. She taught me to be assertive and to ask for what I wanted. I feel truly blessed to have been of service to such an extraordinary woman.

Life Lesson from the Chair: The smallest acts of kindness, performed in quiet humility, always speak the loudest.

Until next haircut…

Helen: A Senior Who Let Her Spirit Soar

Helen was an older client who had been with me ever since 1974, when I was fresh out of hairdressing school. One day, she told me there were two things she'd always wanted to do before she died.

When I asked what those things might be, she said, "The first was to go to a strip club and see a male stripper!"

I howled with laughter at this spry senior! She just smiled slyly. "Did that one last month."

I had to know. "And how was it?" She said, "Ah, it was no big deal."

"The other thing I want to do is fly in a small airplane over the Niagara area and Dunnville where I grew up and see my house."

I thought I could help her with that dream. My husband, Dave, is a private pilot and he has a small plane. When I suggested he might take her up one day she agreed that would be great.

Not long after, Helen's daughter came for an appointment. When she told me she and her family were planning a party to celebrate her Mom's 80th birthday, I told her about Helen's wish to fly.

From the Hairdresser's Chair

I offered to make up a gift certificate for an hour's plane ride. My husband would only charge for the fuel.

"That's perfect!" she said excitedly. "We had no idea what to get her!"

Next time Helen came to see me, she was telling me all about her upcoming party. She was really looking forward to it. She said, "It's not every day you turn 80, you know!" She was proud of her age and accomplishments, so far.

She had raised five children, had nine grandchildren and was a member of the Ladies' Auxiliary at the Legion, where she had been a past-president. She volunteered her time for the Literacy Foundation and she also helped with Meals on Wheels.

She played cards weekly with her friends. Helen loved to hook rugs and many family members had received her beautiful rugs as Christmas gifts.

I could hardly wait to hear how she reacted to getting her gift certificate for her dream plane ride. Helen's daughter decided that flying would be the theme, with little airplanes for the party and cake decorations.

Helen had a wonderful time at her party and was thrilled with the idea of going up in the plane. She'd heard many stories of where Dave and I had flown over the years, so she felt confident going up with him.

But it didn't happen until about six months later, because Helen was ill for some time. Finally, the big day came. Many of Helen's family members came to the Niagara District Airport with her.

She stood beside the plane with my husband to have her picture taken. Without hesitation she climbed in, put on her headset, and they taxied out to the runway.

They took off and headed south. After a beautiful, bird's eye view of Niagara Falls, they flew to Fort Erie and did a quick circuit over the Peace Bridge. Then they followed Lake Erie to Dunnville, Helen's hometown.

They found the house she grew up in, and Helen snapped some pictures.

My husband let her fly the plane for a moment, just to get the feel of it. He gave her a quick lesson: keep it straight and level, watch the attitude indicator, make sure the wings are horizontal to the horizon and you're not climbing or descending. She did just fine!

Helen was loving every minute of the flight, so Dave kept going. He flew over the Welland Canal, then did a full circle up to Hamilton, over the

From the Hairdresser's Chair

Burlington Skyway and back along Lake Ontario before landing in Niagara.

Helen was glowing with excitement when they landed. Her family came running over to greet her. Grinning from ear to ear, she yelled, "I flew the plane and we didn't even crash! I took lots of pictures."

Her next hair appointment, I enjoyed seeing the photos from her flight. I asked her, "So. Now that you've been to a strip club and had your flight, what's next?"

She simply said, "I'm good, I'm happy. I'm content. Life is great!"

Helen passed away at the age of 83. At the funeral home, there was a picture of her, proudly standing in front of the airplane with a big smile on her face.

That day had meant so much to her – the fulfilment of a lifelong dream. We can all take a page from Helen's book of life.

Life Lesson from the Chair: Set some goals and revel in them when you achieve them. But never forget to enjoy the journey. What do you want to do in the time you have?

Until next haircut…

Sandy Has No Complaints

Sandy has always worked in the corporate world where she manages a number of people in her division. She loves her profession and is very career-driven. When I noticed that the stress of her job was starting to wear her down, I told her she needed to refresh and rejuvenate herself.

She agreed that her energy and mood had been dragging lately and admitted she needed a lift. By her next appointment, one had come to her!

Her company was offering to pay for its managers to take a course called, *The Power of Personal Development in the Workplace*. She'd heard good things about it, knew it was expensive and deeply appreciated that the company would pay for it. They even offered a bonus to any employee who completed the four-week training!

Sandy was surprised to learn she was the only one who had signed up. But she was thrilled and couldn't wait to start improving her skills, both at work and in her personal life.

The first Monday evening of the course, the participants determined their goals for the four-week duration and committed to taking three actions each day. The focus was to handle people more professionally, perform as a persuasive communicator, and be a creative problem solver.

From the Hairdresser's Chair

Sandy also learned about the power of words and the language used to communicate with employees.

She knew negative or disengaged employees are less productive, more disruptive and can poison the corporate culture. She discovered that most people focus on what they don't want and don't like. She explained to me that people use negative words all day long. In fact, most people complain an average of 70 times a day!

Her first homework assignment was to go back to work and not complain. She thought, "Well, that's easy. I hardly ever complain."

Sandy had a big wake-up call! She arrived at work at 8:30 and found herself to be very quiet. As the day progressed, a co-worker asked, "Are you feeling okay?" She replied she felt great and had a very productive morning. Lunchtime came and the managers went out for Thai food.

At the restaurant, she found herself quiet again, not adding much to the conversation. After lunch, another co-worker asked, "Are you mad about something?" Sandy's unusual silence had made her think perhaps she'd said or done something wrong.

Sandy didn't want her friends and colleagues to worry, so she told them about her homework. She felt a bit embarrassed to find she was part of a group that complained 70 times a day or more! She challenged all the women to go one day without complaining and see what happened.

Everyone in the office got on board. No complaining, blaming, justifying or being defensive.

After four weeks, the employees, supervisors and managers were more balanced in the workplace and in their personal lives. People were smiling more often, their stress level was lower and customers were being treated well. You could see - and hear - the difference in the workplace.

Sandy's story prompted me to share the "no complaining" exercise with many people I know. Just try it and see what it can do for you!

Life Lesson from the Chair: *Stop complaining and you'll have far less to complain about.*

Until next haircut…

Orma on What Makes a Relationship Great

Standing by my chair at the salon, I hear many stories about my clients' relationships. Whether couples are married or single, in love or in crisis, in a new or an old relationship, I find most people focus on what is *not* working and what they *don't* like in their relationships.

"My husband works too much, I get no help."
"My wife is always running the kids somewhere."
"Sex...what's that? I can't remember the last time."
"My partner spends too much money."

When I chat with people in my chair about what's important to them in a relationship, my suggestion is to have them make a list of what they DO want and have their partner do the same.

Once both are clear on what they want in their relationship, I suggest they move into what I call the two Cs: Communication and Compromise. Just sit down and talk about it. Both of you must compromise. It always works for my husband and me.

One afternoon, I had an elderly client named Orma coming in for her hair appointment. I decided to ask her opinion on what makes a great relationship.

I watched her carefully descend the two flights of stairs to my salon promptly at 2:00 o'clock. I thought, "She's in great shape for someone 89 years old." She's spry and witty, yet at the same time, she can be so sweet and calming. Orma is a petite woman, not even five feet tall.

She always gives me a big hug when she arrives. She's barely up to my armpits! She's my oldest client. I've been doing her hair for 38 years. She always comes into the salon with a big smile on her face. But this day, she was excited to announce it was her anniversary. She and Tommy had been married for 65 years!

What a life those two have had! They had been retired for 25 years and had been travelling ever since, for ten months of the year in their motor home. They travelled all across Canada in the warm months and headed south into the U.S. for the winter. They never stayed too long in one spot; maybe a few weeks, and off they would go.

They would come home for a month in the spring and another month in the fall. Orma always made sure to have her hair done while she was home. So for years, I only saw her twice a year, in April and November.

A year or so ago they decided to sell the motor home. At age 89, Tommy was ready to settle in at home. The two of them were always together. Tommy dropped her off to get her hair done, then headed off to the bookstore to find another book to add to his collection.

So it was especially important to ask on this special anniversary day, "What makes a great relationship, Orma? If you could give me two words what would they be?"

Well, her words were different than mine, but just as important.

Orma said, "Love and trust." She then hesitated before adding, "And you must first love yourself and accept yourself for who you are. Your relationship with your partner can be very deep and rewarding when you love yourself first."

This was a great answer from the retired schoolteacher. She explained, "Trusting and being honest with your partner and sharing everything in his or her life is a must. Tommy and I share everything."

She smiled and said, "It hasn't all been that rosy, though. We've had our struggles, too. You know, we have a rule that we never go to bed mad." She added, "And we still sleep in the same bed! Many of my friends have separate bedrooms." She chuckled, "You call that a marriage?"

"Hmmm", I thought, "There's still some passion for this gal." I liked her answers, so now we have Communication, Compromise, Love and Trust.

When I asked her, "What else?" she came up with Commitment, Passion and Intimacy. Imagine! At 89 years old, she still feels passion for her Tommy!

We both agreed. If you're missing any of these seven components of a marriage, you're not truly experiencing the relationship at its fullest. She commented, "Think about it. Say the husband is not doing well at work and he keeps this from his wife. He is breaking the intimacy and trust of the relationship and now she wonders why he is depressed or withdrawn."

Orma said, "Trusting, sharing and communicating with each other are so important." I loved her advice.

A little while ago, Orma came to see me and said that she had lost her soul mate. Tommy had passed away at the age of 92. However, Orma felt so blessed to have had 66 years of the most fulfilling and rewarding marriage she could ever have dreamed of.

She'll miss Tommy tremendously, and will forever hold all those precious memories deep in her heart.

Life Lesson from the Chair: Orma was right. If you don't learn how to love and forgive yourself first, how can you expect others to love and forgive you? Happiness is an inside job!

Until next haircut...

From the Hairdresser's Chair

Karen on Life's Little Pleasures and Guilty Secrets

Do you remember *I Love Lucy* in the early 60s? Back then, the TV show was on three times a day. I'd watch it after school, one show every half hour starting at 4:00 o'clock.

Did Lucy and Ethel hide things from their husbands? You bet they did! Most of the shows I remember were all about Lucy keeping some kind of secret from Ricky, because she knew she'd get in trouble.

Did we pick up some of that secrecy from Lucy? Why do women feel compelled to hide it from their husbands when they spend money on themselves? Is it buried deep in our subconscious?

We've all heard the story about buying something new to wear and putting it in our closet for a number of weeks. At last, we put it on and our hubby asks, predictably, "Is that new?" And we can say, "Oh no, it's been in my closet for ages."

Many years ago, I had a client named Jeannie. She would come to my salon every eight weeks or so for highlights and a haircut. Back then, we didn't have debit so she would write me a cheque. For some reason, she always wanted to give me half in cash and the rest in a cheque.

I didn't think much of it until one day, after doing this several times, she seemed slightly embarrassed as she hesitantly explained that it was easier than explaining to her husband why it costs so much to get her hair done.

She said, "When he goes for a haircut, he's in and out in twenty minutes and it costs him $15.00. When he sees the cheque book, with half the amount I actually pay for my hair, I get no complaints and it just makes life easier." Then she quietly added, "If he knew what I spent on my hair, he would kill me!"

"Doesn't he wonder why you're at the salon for more than two hours?" I asked her.

"Oh, no," she said, "he's never figured that one out."

That was back in the early nineties. Now, it is twenty years later, and to my surprise, something similar happened today.

Rachel came in for her colour and cut during the day, while her husband was at work. She mentioned she was going to the spa on Friday night and was going to let her husband think she was getting her hair done then. That way, he'd be babysitting the kids. She seemed to feel guilty about two visits in a week to the salon and the spa.

From the Hairdresser's Chair

I asked, "But won't he notice your hair's been done when you go home today?"

"No," she replied, "he'll just think I washed it!"

Frankly, I was puzzled. When I think of these two women, it makes me wonder why we sometimes feel the need to hide our personal pleasures of pampering like some dirty secret. Men think nothing of making large purchases for their garage, or hockey equipment, or golf and gym membership.

What were these two women telling me about their relationship and self-esteem? Isn't honesty at the foundation of a great marriage? Shouldn't women feel worthy and deserving of life's pleasures?

Lucy and Ethel – you didn't do us much good back in the 60s, with your hiding and conniving! Maybe we shouldn't have laughed quite as much as we did.

Life Lesson from the Chair: We all deserve to be good to ourselves guilt-free; men and women.

Until next haircut...

Rena and Patty Discover the Healing Power of a Hug

My Aunt Rena and Cousin Patty have also been my clients for 40 years. When I was in hairdressing school, I'd go to their home and practice. They trusted me!

The bonus to doing your relatives' hair is that you get to see them every month and keep in touch. We don't have to wait for a family reunion. Even though our family is quite large, we're very close-knit.

Aunt Rena eventually had to go into a nursing home, as her Alzheimer's was nearing the final stages. She could no longer come to get her hair done with me. I still went to visit her, taking my Mom to see her sister every other week.

When Patty heard about this book I was writing, she asked if she could contribute her story of her Mom, my Aunt Rena. Of course I said yes! So these are her words. (This would be a good time to grab a box of Kleenex…)

> Alzheimer's is a progressive, degenerative disease of the brain, which causes thinking and memory to become gravely impaired. It's one of the most common forms of dementia and is extremely misunderstood by family members and friends.
>
> When my Mom was first diagnosed with this horrible disease, the doctors tried to

prevent it from worsening with medications that would help slow the disease process. There is NO cure. Watching our precious Mom slip away, day by day over a period of about ten years, was like having someone slowly die piece by piece.

There were many happy times and sad times. There was so much frustration within our family because people did not realize that Mom wasn't simply forgetful. She often phoned the same person ten times a day, with the same questions and conversation.

I'll always remember the night she gave up her driver's license and how petrified she was. My daughter had invited her over to have dinner with her and her new fiancé. Mom got lost driving to her home and ended up in another city. She cried her eyes out at the side of the road before she could ask for help and find her way home.

She never drove again.

Alzheimer's disease eventually affects all aspects of a person's life: how you think, feel and act. Since individuals are affected differently, it's difficult to predict the symptoms each person will have, the order in which they will appear or the speed of the disease's progression.

We moved our Mom into our own home for two years to help her with medication programming, geriatric assessment strategies and to provide her the quality of life she so deserved as she was afraid now to be alone.

My husband is a true saint. He loved my Mom and she loved him, so this was an easy transition. She could no longer make decisions. Simple tasks were so stressful and she began to feel depressed.

She constantly asked for her husband, our Dad who, unfortunately, had passed away at the age of 64. Mom prayed every night to him and God to ask for their help and peace. She went to church as often as she could with my sister and me.

I remember a period of about six months when my Mom knew she was 'not well' and this was her greatest fear. She cried many nights and often called herself stupid because she couldn't remember. She talked about wishing she would die, rather than be like this.

Those were the hardest months of all.

My Mom had watched her own mother slip away from this same dreadful disease. Mom needed support and constant reminders of how much we loved her, how smart she was her whole life. Most of all, she needed our constant presence to help her with her thoughts and memory recall.

Having her at our home was an awesome experience for her and for our family. After two years, though, she became so dependent that we could no longer provide the care she needed and she moved into a retirement home where she tried her best to be independent.

During the eight years following her diagnosis, many great things happened for my Mom. Her sisters were amazing. Thank goodness for our family and friends!

Mom's friends from church drove her places. She attended the hockey games that had always been her passion. She went to family parties and took trips to Florida, New York and even Winnipeg for a family wedding.

She was lucky enough to have taken two Caribbean cruises with her sister and the help of my brother. However, many of these events were well chaperoned because she could barely carry out the activities of daily living.

Mom was blessed to see her grandchildren grow up, and further honoured to have four great-grandchildren who absolutely love her.

After ten years, she no longer knew who we were although at times we had a glimmer of hope that she recognized us.

If I were to offer advice, I'd say that you should never ask someone with Alzheimer's disease questions like: Who am I? Do you know what day it is? How old are you?

This is so frustrating to them. It's much better to say, "Hey! I came to visit you today and it's Tuesday. I'm your daughter and I want to wish you a Happy 81st Birthday and tell you how much I love you!"

Then you'll be rewarded with a smile and bright eyes shining, because she's not being asked to recall something she simply can't.

Many people were afraid to visit my Mom. They weren't sure what to do, what to say or how to help. It's not really their fault; it's very, very difficult. But I wanted to share my story with anyone who might be going through something similar.

One day at work, I had a horrible migraine. I was under severe pressure from deadlines and felt I might be sick. Luckily, my Mom's room in long-term care was very close to where I work. I couldn't take looking at my computer any longer or talking on the phone.

I was feeling physically drained, so I went to visit Mom. When I got to her room, she was sitting looking out the window with a very blank stare on her face. She was wheelchair-bound and had a table strapped in front of her so she would not attempt to walk and fall.

I approached her softly and said, "Hi Mom. It's me – your favourite daughter, Patty!" That's how I always joked with her so she would not have to remember my name.

From the Hairdresser's Chair

She smiled and said, "Hello. How are you?"

I replied, "I don't feel well. I have a terrible migraine and I just needed to see you. How about a nice hug? I really need it."

She said, "Sure."

So I removed the table that was holding her in her chair, and I leaned down for my hug. She didn't know how to move her arms; they hung limp at her side.

I said, "Mom - I need a big hug." I took her arms and wrapped them around me as I did the same to her. I said, "Squeeze tight." – and she did! All of a sudden, it came back to her. She held me tighter and tighter. We could both instantly feel relief and peace.

We hugged each other for about a minute, and when we both let go, she kissed my cheek and said, "I love you." I began to cry softly, but didn't want her to know. As I stood up, my headache was instantly gone, and the sickness had disappeared. In fact, I felt so much relief and calmness that I was taken aback.

I looked at my Mom's eyes and it was like we could see each other's souls. For a moment, I was shaken. I whispered, "Thank you Mom. You made me feel so much better. That was the best hug I have ever had in my entire life!"

She replied in a clear voice, "We need to do that more often, then."

After that, I hugged her every time I saw her. I'd hold her tight, and always breathe a prayer, 'Thank you, God, for giving me this great gift.'

Whenever I felt stressed, tired, worn out or 'just because' – I'd hug my Mom. We didn't have to say anything – we just knew. The whole world felt better and I knew that she did, too.

So to all those people out there who think that just because someone has Alzheimer's disease, their life is over, IT'S NOT TRUE! They can make a difference in your life with a hug and you can make a significant impact on theirs. Even if you cannot see it – you can both feel it.

So HUG AWAY and spread the word about the unlimited potential of a simple hug!

Karen here. My Aunt Rena passed away two weeks after this story was written. She died peacefully in the nursing home.

Life Lesson from the Chair: Anne Frank once wrote that we all have something to give, even if it's just a kindness. Hugs are such a kindness, with proven healing power, too.

Until next haircut...

Sharon, Lois and Karen Reflect on Birthing Babies

Women love to talk about the birth of their babies and compare stories. Was yours easy? Painful? A nightmare? Too long? All of the above? No matter how it went, holding that dear little bundle of creation in your arms was the most amazing, joyful time of our lives.

Years ago, in the '80s, I had a client named Lois who shared with me that her daughter, Sharon, was expecting her third child. Sharon had always amazed me.

Fit and energetic, Sharon jogged daily and played basketball twice a week. She sat on the Board of Directors for a local charity and volunteered as a Big Sister.

She only served fresh food to her family, stopping at the market on her way home from work every day. Meals were always freshly prepared and even her baby foods were homemade! Sharon and her husband were both very health-conscious. He was also active in the community and very helpful around the house. Somehow, they managed to balance work, family, sports, community contribution and time with each other.

Her previous pregnancies had been a breeze, so I wasn't surprised to hear about another baby coming along. Seven months into her pregnancy, Sharon was still running daily and considering a 5K race. Her doctor gave his permission, because it was normal for her, and she was so healthy. She barely even showed!

Lois told me she'd be driving the 90 minutes to watch the other children when Sharon went into labour. She chuckled, "I hope I can get there in time, because her last babies came so quickly; within a few hours."

The baby's due date happened to be Halloween night. Sharon's two young girls were in costume: a fairy, covered with glitter and a magic wand in hand and a princess with a beautiful tiara. They were very excited to go out trick-or-treating. Sharon had spent the evening taking them door to door; her husband had stayed home to shell out.

After tucking the trick-or-treaters into bed at 9:00 o'clock, Sharon felt a sudden labour pain and thought she'd better let her Mom know. Lois got the call around 10:00 and immediately got into 'grandma mode', to come babysit. In the meantime, Sharon had called her neighbour to come watch the children, because she knew things were happening too fast to wait for Lois.

Her husband sped them off to the hospital, remembering how fast their first two babies had arrived. Suddenly, Sharon's water broke and the baby's head became engaged! No cell phones back then. He couldn't call for help. He carefully ran a red light, raced around a corner and roared into the Emergency parking area.

Running into the Emergency, he called frantically for help. He didn't want to deliver this baby himself! Sharon couldn't move. The attendants quickly lifted her onto a stretcher and whisked her into the hospital. Just four minutes later, their little Natasha was born.

By this time, Lois had arrived to relieve the neighbour. The phone rang and she heard her son-in-law's voice. "It's a girl! Labour and delivery were fast. Mom and baby are fine!"

Lois checked on the grandkids, then settled in for the night. She expected a busy morning, getting them off to school then going to visit her new granddaughter. Sharon was so fit and healthy, her delivery so fast and easy with no stitches and just an hour of labour, with the help of a midwife, she could well have had the child at home as many are these days.

Isn't it funny how some things go back to the way they used to be? My mother and her sisters were all born at home on the dining room table. In those days, the doctor would come to the house to deliver the infant and a new mom would stay in bed for ten days to recover.

Today, women are up and moving around within hours after a delivery. Sharon convinced her doctor to let her go home a few hours after the baby was born. Keep in mind this was in the 1980s, when women typically stayed in the hospital for at least five days to recover.

Sharon was back home by 4:00 o'clock in the morning! This was unheard-of. Her children woke up to Mom and a new baby sister sitting on the couch while Grandma made their breakfast. Does it get any better than that?

If only everyone's babies were delivered that quickly. My first-born took ten hours of hard labour, two hours of pushing and even then forceps were needed to bring my 9-lb, 10-oz bundle of joy into the world. 50 stitches!

My second child was easier. Labour started through the night. I arrived at the hospital on the shift change at 7:45 am and things happened fast. I told the nurse I had to push and she calmly said the doctor would be in soon.

However, my son's birth had really paved the way for my daughter's grand entrance. Again, I called the nurse to say I was pushing, and to her surprise, there was the baby's head! Things started moving fast and my daughter was born by 9:00 am. Hers was an easy birth, but I still stayed in the hospital for five days because that's how long they kept you back then.

From the Hairdresser's Chair

Life Lesson from the Chair: *It doesn't matter if you're giving birth to a baby, a business or an idea. The labour involved may be intense, painful, quick or all of the above. But the joy of the final result is well worth it.*

Until next haircut…

Janet Knows Diamonds Are NOT a Girl's Best Friend

We've all heard that man's best friend is the one with four legs and a tail, who's always happy to see you no matter what. Who sticks by your side and listens to every word you say, whether you're happy or miserable.

When you think of woman's best friend, you probably think of girlfriends spending a day at the spa or shopping with your sister and spending too much money. Or maybe of a close friend you call when you're upset and just need to talk.

While all of those could be true, I'm sharing the story of my client, Janet's, best friend.

Janet is a divorcée who has a 13-year-old son named Derek and an adorable little dog named Cocoa. She brought her to my salon one time to show me. Cocoa is really tiny, cute and very well behaved. I told Janet that Cocoa was welcome any time she came to get her hair done.

One time, Janet's company was sending her on a business trip to Toledo. Her sister, Margie, was happy to look after Derek and Cocoa. Margie loves dogs and Derek would be in school all day, playing sports afterward. Neither the boy nor the dog would be a problem for her.

From the Hairdresser's Chair

Margie and Cocoa set off in the car to pick up Derek at the park after his game. It was getting dark. Margie stopped the car, stepped out for a second and yelled to let Derek know she was there with the car, waiting.

As the two drove home, they realized that Cocoa wasn't there! She must have jumped out in the few seconds when Margie had opened the door to call to Derek. They raced back to the park to get her.

By then, it was very dark. They searched everywhere, spending hours, but couldn't find Cocoa. "What will I ever tell Janet?" Margie worried. They went home, called the SPCA and left a frantic message about the dog. Then Margie had to make the dreaded call to her sister.

Janet was devastated. She felt hopeless and helpless, stuck in Toledo. Margie assured her they were doing everything they could to locate her dog.

As soon as day broke, Margie was out with a team of people to find Cocoa. They posted signs everywhere and went door to door. Meanwhile, back in Toledo, Janet was a basket case, sitting helpless.

She got on her computer and notified everyone she knew, asking them to go out and help Margie search.

The search team continued to grow, but still no Cocoa could be found. The SPCA was called and reported that no one appeared to have found her.

Finally, at 3:00 o'clock that afternoon, the SPCA called Margie to say that someone had her dog, but hadn't left their phone number.

Janet got the news that someone had her precious Cocoa. Although relieved, she couldn't help but wonder if she'd ever see her dog again.

By 7:00 pm, there was still no word from the man who had contacted the SPCA. The dog park was still full of people looking for Cocoa when an elderly man in a red Corvette showed up.

Janet's friend's daughter held up a picture of Cocoa and asked the newcomer if he had seen her. He said, "Yes! The dog was at his home." He invited her into his car to take her there. But her mother told her she wasn't hopping into a stranger's car!

An older friend of Janet's offered to go instead and off they went. They pulled up to a big house and in she went. No fear! She called out Cocoa's name and the little dog came running, hopping into her arms.

Tears of relief and gratitude filled her eyes. She couldn't wait to call Janet and head back to the park to celebrate with the search party.

From the Hairdresser's Chair

Cocoa was fine. The elderly man's wife had just given her a bath and fed her. (We think she might have wanted to keep her). When the red Corvette returned to the dog park, Janet's friend jumped out with Cocoa in her arms and yelled to the searchers for someone to call Janet right away!

When she got the happy news, Janet couldn't stop crying. Cocoa is the joy of her life. Whenever she tells the story of Cocoa's adventure in the salon, we all have tears.

Cocoa goes to the salon and spa with Janet. Cocoa goes shopping at the mall. Cocoa is there to listen whenever Janet is upset.

Life Lesson from the Chair: *Forget about diamonds. A girl's real best friend has four legs and a tail, too!*

Until next haircut...

Betty Survives a Stroke

After having taught kindergarten for many years, Betty was enjoying her retirement. Sewing had always been her passion and she shared it with others by teaching sewing classes ever since she retired.

One morning, when Betty was 72 years old, she suffered a stroke. She had awakened early, gone into the bathroom and was bumping into the walls. She went back to bed.

Getting up a bit later, she noticed her left hand was numb. She dropped everything she picked up.

She went to her doctor's that day and noticed that her left leg was also numb. He was about to send her home then thought better of it. His receptionist took Betty straight to the hospital and she was admitted.

Betty thought, "This can't be happening to me. Only OLD people have strokes!" Hers was a mild one but it still kept her in hospital for over a month.

During that time, I would go to the hospital to cut her hair. Being there was bad enough; not having good hair days made things that much worse! Clients are always so happy to see me when I do my 'hospital rounds'. Even if they don't need a cut or other service, I'll just touch up their hair. Looking better, makes them feel better.

From the Hairdresser's Chair

After her hospital stay, Betty had to go for rehab at another facility. She's a real trooper. It was no time at all before she was coming back to my salon. The feeling has returned to her leg but her left arm and hand hang limp.

The worst part for Betty was losing her independence. It was difficult for her to ask for rides to her appointments. Her license was revoked until the doctor could clear her. When it was time to drive again, she had to take lessons. She needed to learn how to drive with only one hand and arm. Then she had to take a road test.

She worked very hard at it and passed the test. Then she received a prescription for a steering wheel knob that allowed her to turn corners more easily with just one hand.

Although she only regained 20% of the use of her left arm, Betty was very relieved to have her license – and independence – back.

Throughout this ordeal, I never heard Betty complain; she focused on learning to adjust to her unexpected setback. She amazes me with her courage to move forward. Ten years later, she's still making the 30-minute drive to my salon. She's 82!

I told her that she wouldn't hurt my feelings if she wanted to find a hairstylist closer to home. "No." she said. "I don't mind the drive and I like coming here. It's a day out for me. Afterward, I go shopping with my good hair!"

At her last appointment, I asked Betty what her biggest struggle was. She said it was sewing. It takes her much longer to do now, but she found a way to change her technique that was working. She recently made a coat, jacket and many T-shirts!

She continues to mentor her sewing group. They love having her guide them with her expertise.

Betty still goes to physical therapy twice a week. She says it keeps her limber so she can enjoy life to the fullest. When I asked what other challenges she faced, she replied that cooking with one arm can be a chore. And she can no longer play her mandolin.

"If you want to experience how it feels; just try to put a pillow in a pillowcase with only one arm," she suggested. I tried it and she's right! It's next to impossible.

Of course, doing her hair is one of those easy yet difficult tasks. Working together, we found a way for her to manage it, though. She observed that we often don't realize what we have until we lose it. We should all be more grateful for our hands, feet – all our body parts!

Betty has such a positive outlook. Never once did she ask, "Why me?" She continues to make the most out of every day. Every week, she meets up with her fellow teaching retirees who were such a huge support to her during her recovery.

She drives to all her grandson's soccer and hockey games. Betty believes if there's a will, there's a way. I appreciate her positive attitude. I'm inspired by how she survived her stroke and thrived in spite of it.

Life Lesson from the Chair: Singer Joni Mitchell sang, "Don't it always seem to go that you don't know what you've got 'til it's gone?" The teacher in Betty would have granted poetic license to Joni's grammar, but surely she applauds and shares the sentiment!

Until next haircut...

Judy Adopts a New Attitude and a New Daughter

I have a client named Dora whose daughter is in a loving, same-sex relationship. Judy and Amy had been trying to have a baby for quite some time and there were several ways to do it available to them. However, Judy suffers from endometriosis, which greatly reduces her chances of getting pregnant.

Judy spent a lot of time preparing herself for implantation. She ate a very restricted healthy diet, exercised regularly, and had Reiki treatments to clear her body. She even had a spiritual cleansing of her womb.

Eventually, a donor was found. Judy was ready, the doctor was monitoring her closely and the donor could be ready on short notice once Judy started ovulating. The first method they tried was the 'turkey baster', as it's often called. After implantation, Judy would have to lie still for quite some time, hoping an egg would be fertilized.

She prayed every day for this miracle to happen, but month after month, no pregnancy. She was so disappointed. Amy was ready to go the adoption route, but Judy really wanted her own child.

It was hard for Amy to see her partner suffer through her failures to get pregnant. Judy wanted to carry a child; Amy just wanted to have one.

From the Hairdresser's Chair

They decided to try in vitro. It was a very expensive procedure but Judy's longing to have a child would not go away. Looking into it, they discovered the chances of getting pregnant were about fifty percent. After much discussion, the appointments were booked. Judy's eggs were harvested and a suitable donor was found at the sperm bank.

The first month, it didn't take. The second month, Judy was ecstatic to be late with her period. Then, to her great disappointment, it arrived five days later.

She was completely distraught and couldn't get out of bed for two days. Finally, she pulled herself back together and started praying. "God, if I'm not supposed to be a Mom, please take away this yearning."

It didn't go away. She prayed again for this miracle of pregnancy. She was ready, felt cleansed, clear and had strong faith. The pregnancy happened! But it only lasted a couple days. She had an early miscarriage. Devastated beyond belief, she was depressed and lay in bed again for a few days.

Amy said she would go the next time. She prepared mentally, physically and spiritually. Then she was ready. The fourth in vitro took place, but it didn't take. Five times they tried. The expense was enormous, with no pregnancy to show for it.

Dora used to say to her daughter, "Judy, you *will* have a child. You were meant to be a Mom. The baby may just have to come from China, but you *will* be a Mom!"

After all the grief and high hopes, Judy and Amy came to terms with adoption. They turned it over to God, surrendering all their pain, disappointment and heartache. For the first time in years, they both felt at peace.

Deciding that a baby would be wonderful, but a young child would still be a very great blessing, they contacted Family and Children Services. It had been years since they'd been trying to make good on their decision to have a baby before Judy's fortieth birthday.

In November, Family and Children Services called to say they had a two-year-old girl in need of a good home. All the paperwork had been completed so they were all set to become foster parents.

They visited the little girl every day for two weeks and had a sleepover on the weekends.

Two weeks before Christmas, they were granted custody. Judy and Amy were elated at God's gift to them. The tears ran down Dora's cheeks as she shared this wonderful news with me. Six months later, the little one was legally adopted and Dora was so proud to become her Grandma!

From the Hairdresser's Chair

Surrendering was the answer. When Judy was at peace, all the details, people and circumstances came together to bless her and Amy with this beautiful daughter.

Life Lesson from the Chair: *Believe that everything happens for a reason. We may not see it right away, but have faith that He always knows what's best for us and that the universe will unfold exactly as it's meant to.*

Until next haircut...

Janis and Gary: A Stop and Go Relationship

As an executive of a large network marketing company, Janis is a very organized woman and powerful in her field. She's responsible for keeping her huge team on their path to financial independence.

But, she often felt her life was incomplete. She'd been widowed for several years and was ready to start dating, in the hope of eventually settling down.

During an appointment, she told me how she had met a man named Gary. They'd both pulled up to a stoplight, looked across at each other and exchanged smiles. Janis drove to her destination – the local hardware store – and Gary pulled up beside her in the parking lot.

He introduced himself and asked if he might call her sometime to meet for a drink. Although she was surprised at his direct approach, Janis gave him her number.

"There was something very intriguing about him even though, on the outside, he wasn't my type," she told me.

"What do you mean?" I asked her, curious to know.

From the Hairdresser's Chair

"Well, he's very rugged looking. Like a farmer or someone who works with his hands," she replied.

"When I got home from the hardware store," Janis went on, "I Googled him. He owns a Landscape and Garden Center."

She wondered if he would call her. Only a day later, he did! She was surprised how much she was looking forward to talking to him. She told me they'd made a date for the following Friday night. Once she got off the phone with Gary, though, she started to worry about their plans for a dinner date.

"What if I don't like him? What if I get stuck talking to someone I don't like for a few hours?" At first she reconsidered her plans, but decided to follow her initial intuition and keep the date.

Janis discovered that she and Gary had many things in common. They both loved to travel and had visited many of the same destinations. They both had grown children and they each still had one living at home.

At her appointment the next month, they'd had a few more dates and Janis told me excitedly, "He's the one I'm going to marry!" Three more months and many more dates went by. I'd never seen Janis so happy. Every time, she would gush about Gary.

Everything was going great until one summer day. Gary called Janis and told her they needed to talk.

When Janis came to see me next, she told me Gary had broken up with her. She was absolutely devastated.

He told her the relationship was great, but it was moving too quickly for him. He had been married three times before and was nervous about getting into another serious relationship. He just wasn't ready.

Two long weeks went by before Gary realized he had made a huge mistake. He contacted Janis and begged her to take him back. She was very reluctant after having been so hurt. She decided to forgive him and give their relationship another chance.

They had a long talk about their thoughts and feelings. Together, they decided they could get past the disruption in their relationship and agreed to take it slow.

As Grace Cirocco puts it in her best selling book **Take the Step, the Bridge will be There**, "We are all human beings, making mistakes and trying to find our way. We are confused and lost and at times we despair. But we are trying to be found. Forgiveness is the way home. Forgiveness is like a soothing spring that erupts from deep within Mother Earth and bathes everything in its path with Light."

A few years went by, and their relationship was great. But, they were still living separately with no sign of marriage on the horizon. Janis wanted to sell both of their homes, build a new one together and get married, Gary still could not commit.

From the Hairdresser's Chair

Their fourth anniversary of dating was approaching fast and Janis was becoming frustrated with the lack of progression. She told me that she felt she had waited long enough and given Gary all the time he should need. Her children and Gary's had all moved out and still there was no long-term commitment.

During one appointment, Janis seemed particularly frustrated and defeated. I told her that she needed to share how she felt with Gary. It was time for an honest and open discussion of how both were feeling.

Janis needed to tell Gary how important marriage was to her and that she wanted to spend her life with him. Every time she would bring it up, he'd change the subject or brush it off and wanted to talk about it later.

As I was finishing her hair, Janis was in tears. She told me she felt they were perfect together, but she didn't know how much longer she could wait.

My last advice to her that day was to try and focus on all the positive things in their relationship and to talk about what they *did* have together rather than what they didn't have. Janis wiped her tears away and agreed.

She listed off a few of the traits she loved about him the most. He was generous, kind to her family and friends, attentive, supportive and respectful. They had a solid relationship.

Finally, as year six approached, Gary proposed. He'd planned a very special weekend. He'd booked a weekend getaway up at Blue Mountain. He took her to a wonderful restaurant.

Back at the chalet, as they sat in front of a beautiful fire, Gary told her she was his soul mate, best friend and the love of his life. He got down on one knee, with tears in his eyes, and proposed. Of course she said YES!

I got a phone call the next day. She couldn't wait until her next hair appointment. As I said, "Hello?" Janis yelled into the phone, "I got my ring!"

She had received a beautiful sapphire and diamond engagement ring. I was so happy for my client and friend. I told her good things come to those who wait and she agreed. She realized that the time needed to be right for both of them. Even though Gary took a little longer to be ready, it didn't mean he loved her any less.

Relationships can be difficult but it is important to have honest and open communication through any obstacles that we encounter. In order for Janis and Gary's relationship to grow and be successful, they both needed to be aware of what the other person needed.

Janis needed to feel commitment from Gary and Gary needed Janis to be patient with him. It's important to remember that relationships will grow stronger each time you jump over a hurdle or push past a problem.

It's amazing to think that it all started with a smile at a stoplight. Now they are living a beautiful life together.

Life Lesson from the Chair: *Love and forgiveness are two powerful emotions that bring us joy and feelings of peace. When you give your attention, energy and focus to what you like and appreciate, you'll find that many more things to like and appreciate. Like definitely attracts like.*

Until next haircut...

Karen Remembers Carl the Fisherman

I have so many wonderful summertime memories from my childhood! Sometimes it's hard to recollect just one in particular. But, I'll never forget the year I turned twelve.

It was 1968. My Dad, Carl, loved being on the water. Not only did we live near the Great Lakes, we also spent many summer family vacations up north in the Muskokas, renting cottages on Mary Lake.

That summer, Dad decided it was time for me to learn how to pilot the family boat. I also had to master the skill of towing a water skier. Him, of course!

My Dad was totally selfless, always teaching others to ski, and giving up his time day after day so the rest of us could learn. As a result, he himself remained an average skier. He was, however, an avid fisherman and he shared those secrets with us, too.

Dad loved his boat. Just a big kid at heart. At the end of the day, if he wasn't too tired, he'd even take the adults for an evening cruise.

At home in Fort Erie, my parents lived just a few minutes from the Niagara River. With its fast current, Dad made sure we all learned how to swim at a very young age. My three siblings and I took swimming lessons for many years. Dad would test our skills against the swift currents of the mighty Niagara.

We often launched the boat in the river, but always headed south to the calmer waters of Lake Erie for our boating adventures.

Fishing was always best in Lake Erie, near Port Colborne. We'd usually catch perch and pickerel that Dad would clean and Mom would cook. She often came with us because she enjoyed the boat almost as much as we did. If she tired of fishing, she'd just relax with a book in the warm sun and balmy breeze.

Dad enjoyed his life to the fullest, always including his family whenever he could. His zest for life touched many people in a warm and loving way. His health was very important to him; he was disciplined and very fit, exercising every day and walking at least 40 miles a week.

In the spring of 1997, we celebrated Dad's 65th birthday and surprised him with a family party. My brother flew home from Alberta - his gift to make this occasion memorable. Dad was surprised and the party was a huge success.

The whole year was eventful! My brother, his wife and their children came home again that summer for a great week at the cottage. The grandkids loved to fish, and Dad taught them how to put a worm on the hook (definitely not my cup of tea!).

As fall approached, it came time to winterize the boat once again and put it away. It had been a wonderful summer with his boat and Dad neatly tucked it away to await the next spring.

He decided to go visit my brother and see his grandkids. They were growing up too fast! Mom wanted to wait until spring because they'd all just been home to visit. But, for some reason, Dad insisted he wanted to enjoy the breathtaking scenery and fresh mountain air of Canmore, Alberta.

It turned out to be his last trip. My folks had only been home from Canmore for a few weeks when we received a phone call we never expected. Dad had suffered a massive heart attack!

We were in shock and disbelief. I remember calling Dad's sisters and they couldn't comprehend what I was telling them about their brother, Carl's condition. To them and to my cousins, Uncle Carl was the picture of health.

My Mom, two sisters, my brother and I sat by his side for six long days, watching him fight for the life he loved so much. Floods of relatives and friends streamed through that hospital room to show their love and respect for this man. He fought until he could fight no longer.

From the Hairdresser's Chair

We buried him at the end of November.

None of this made sense to us. This wasn't supposed to happen. My Dad's parents had lived to be 87 and 93! It was a tough Christmas and winter that year. I remember all of us helping Mom adjust to her new life. It broke our hearts. Spring finally came, but sadness still hung in the air.

Soon enough, it was time to deal with Dad's boat. No one in the family wanted to sell it, but Mom knew it was the right thing and we'd have to do it.

My husband, Dave, prepared to put it on the market. Emotions ran high as he uncovered Dad's pride and joy. Fond memories came rushing back to us in a flood. The boat seemed to be waiting for the usual summertime family fun. My heart ached when the "for sale" sign went up.

Many people came by to look at this special boat that meant so much to us. There was a lot of interest. After about three days of showing Dad's boat, a grey-haired man in his sixties stopped by for a look.

He told Dave he had just discovered he could retire earlier than planned so he thought he would buy a fishing boat. He lived near Fort Erie and thought it would be the perfect way to start his retirement. After thoroughly looking over the boat and all its gear, he declared it was exactly what he'd always wanted.

We just knew he would appreciate our family boat for its true value. Dad's boat would find a good home and sail off on new adventures. As the stranger drew out his cheque book, Dave asked him his name.

He looked up and said, "My name is Carl!" With shivers coursing through him, Dave told him the astounding news that the former owner, his father-in-law, was also named Carl. "I think this was meant to be then." the new owner remarked as he finished writing his cheque.

To me it was incredible, yet perfectly fitting, that our Dad's beloved boat would be passed along to a "new" Carl. I truly believe things happen for good reason. Perhaps there would be another generation of grandchildren casting fishing lines or water-skiing behind our family's boat.

The rest of our family was thrilled to hear that another Carl had just purchased their Carl's boat!

Life Lesson from the Chair: *Don't worry too much about your legacy. Our everyday kindnesses and actions have a way of showing up in others' lives in ways we don't expect or may never know.*

Until next haircut…

From the Hairdresser's Chair

Maya: Made in China

When Sandy told me she was studying Chinese at night school, I was really surprised. "It's a very difficult language to learn," she confided. "So far, my average is in the 30s! But, I thought it would be interesting."

A few months later, I discovered her true motivation. She had decided to adopt a little baby from China. I was thrilled for her!

Divorced and single for many years, she wanted children and had been trying to get pregnant through artificial insemination for a year and a half. After three disappointing miscarriages, her fertility doctor said it just wasn't working. The procedure was very expensive.

He gently suggested that, if she could afford the $20,000 or so, Sandy should call the Children's Bridge Agency in Ottawa and look into adopting a child from China.

Sandy felt she needed to do it soon. The process involved about 18 months and a lot of red tape, especially with the Canadian and Chinese governments. Then in her mid-forties, Sandy had the added challenge of being an American citizen, living in Canada. She had to become a Canadian citizen first.

While the process normally takes 10 months, Sandy's determination had it taken care of within 10 weeks! She contacted her MP, called the Minister of Immigration in Ottawa and had many people working for her to get things done.

She was sworn in as a Canadian citizen on a Monday. Two days later, on the Wednesday, was the cut-off day for the next group to adopt from China! Sandy had to get her paperwork sent off to Ottawa. She discovered her doctor had missed one question so she scrambled and got it done. With only an hour to spare, she got her papers in order and submitted, making it into this group!

The fees were very expensive and Sandy had exhausted all her savings over the past two years, paying for her fertility treatments. Fortunately, the National Bank offered an international adoption loan at a very low interest rate.

On December 21, she received the first picture of her baby from China. She was 11 months old at the time. Sandy named her Maya. She met with many of the adopting families before leaving for China. She met families who had previously adopted, as well.

The time was fast approaching to leave and Sandy was busy preparing for it.

She had become friends with a single mom named Lianne, who had already adopted a child. She told

From the Hairdresser's Chair

Sandy she'd need some help. "When I went, I took both of my parents and my sister, Kim." Lianne said.

"Well, I'm going alone," Sandy told her. "No one can afford to go with me and I can't afford to pay anyone's way."

When Lianne's sister, Kim, heard about this, she decided to do some fundraising in her hometown of San Francisco. Kim knew how much help her sister had needed when she and her parents had taken the same trip.

When Sandy heard about Kim's fundraising on her behalf, she was very surprised and pleased. Kim was holding car washes and bake sales to raise money for her, a stranger! People were making large donations: $50.00 for a car wash or $20.00 for a cookie. Sandy received a cheque for $1200.00 US!

Sandy felt so blessed for this wonderful gift from Lianne's sister, whom she'd never met. Now she and her friend, Angelina, could go together. Unfortunately, just before they bought her ticket, Angelina had to have emergency surgery and couldn't make the trip.

Sandy was going alone after all.

However, she used the extra money to make the trip easier. She bought a seat for the baby to rest in on the way home. The extra funds also provided lots of tip money for her to enlist help at the airports or wherever she went. Sandy would just wave a $20.00 bill and get lots of eager helpers!

She was so grateful to Kim for raising the money to help her. What a compassionate sister Lianne had!

During the trip, Sandy met another single mother en-route to China to adopt. Andrea was from Ottawa but they met in Vancouver, on Valentine's Day. The two stayed in Shanghai for three days of sightseeing and to get some rest before leaving to see their babies.

The rest of the 30 families arrived on February 19 then they all departed together for Jiangxi Province, where the babies were waiting.

Maya arrived in Sandy's arms, dressed in a blue snowsuit but layered in soiled clothes inside it. Everyone mingled for a few minutes to look at each other's babies. By that time, all the parents had bonded and emotions were running high.

Most of the babies just cried. Maya didn't. She was just curious.

The new parents were cautioned against bathing their babies; it was too much trauma for one day. Sandy ignored that advice, bathing Maya immediately and putting fresh clothes on her, which Maya seemed to enjoy.

From the Hairdresser's Chair

She had some help because a few families had to wait until the next day for their babies.

For most of the group, though, the next day was Adoption Day. They were to bring crisp, clean currency to the court. If the bills were wrinkled, they had to be ironed!

It was now February 20 and the adoptive parents had to stay in the Province for one week, waiting for the babies' passports. Then, once they arrived, they flew to Beijing to complete the medical examination and Canadian paperwork that would give them a visa, allowing the babies to enter Canada.

Maya was 16 pounds and only 26 inches long. She was 13 months old and she couldn't even sit up. She barely left her crib and had never eaten solid food, only formula.

Home in Canada, Sandy made a doctor's appointment to have Maya assessed. She was told that Maya was developmentally delayed. Sandy refused to accept that. She could see in Maya's eyes that there was more to this wee child than the doctors were giving her credit for.

Sandy was on parental leave for nine months. She worked with this little one like no other Mom could have. Maya had lots of therapy. An occupational therapist and public nurse came to the house twice a week. She also took Maya to a physical therapist.

I remember the first time Sandy brought Maya to my salon. She could only sit up with a pillow behind her back. She was afraid of textures, because she had never left her crib. She couldn`t pivot around when she first started standing. Therapy helped her to learn, and finally, at 22 months she walked.

Her first words came after age two and then something happened between the ages of two and three. Maya was speaking in entire paragraphs! The doctors were amazed that this was the same child. Sandy went to enroll her in Junior Kindergarten at age three.

She was told that Maya was too young. She had to be able to count to 30 and list more than one word for each letter of the alphabet.

When they tested her, they discovered that Maya could count to 200 and had no problem with her ABCs! She started JK that September, at the tender age of three.

After Senior Kindergarten, Maya had to change schools. Enrolling in the Catholic school system, she was asked to repeat SK. Sandy didn't like the idea but it wasn't long before the teachers noticed how well Maya was doing. They moved her up to Grade 1.

Today, Maya is in Grade 10, doing some Grade 11 work. She has grown to be a very compassionate, kind, generous and empathetic young teen. Her mother is so proud of her!

She is wise beyond her years. What a beautiful girl, made in China!

Life Lesson from the Chair: *Every child deserves a chance at life, to be loved and cared for. Thank heaven there are people so patient and willing to welcome these little ones into their hearts, homes and lives.*

Until next haircut...

Dave Gives Three Dads the Best Father's Day Gift Ever!

Father's Day was approaching and, in my salon, many clients were chatting about what they should give their Dad or husband for their special day.

One of them, a woman named Sandra, asked me, "Is there any way you could make a gift certificate for my husband, Ron, to go up for an airplane ride with your husband?"

I said, "Absolutely! Dave would love to take Ron up for an aerial tour of Niagara. Anytime someone wants to pay for the fuel and go for a brief flight, it helps my husband keep current and adds hours to his pilot's log."

By Friday of the Father's Day weekend, I had three flights booked for Dave to take on the Sunday! One client asked, "Are you sure your husband doesn't mind taking mine flying on Father's Day?"

"Are you kidding?" I answered. "For sure he'd much rather be flying than cutting the grass! Flying is his passion. An afternoon in the plane would be the best Father's Day gift he could receive!"

Rebecca is another client who had bought a flight for her husband. She brought her two daughters to the Niagara Airport to watch their Dad enjoy his gift and take pictures.

From the Hairdresser's Chair

They were sitting at a picnic table, watching the plane taxi down the runway when one of the girls started to panic. The door was open on her Dad's side of the plane. When she told the others, they all started jumping up and down to get the attention of Dave and their Dad. They didn't realize that this was perfectly normal. In the summer, it's very warm inside the cockpit of this small airplane. The door's left open while the plane is taxiing so a breeze from the propeller can cool it off a bit. Just before take-off, the pilot will ask the passenger to close and lock the door.

Once the plane started to climb, the girls saw the door was shut. They calmed down and watched it continue.

I wasn't at the airport; I just heard the story when Dave got home. He'd had quite the day!

The first Dad had brought his daughter along for the flight and she'd been as quiet as could be. The second Dad had terrified the teenagers watching on the tarmac! And the third had brought along his son, who was more excited than his Dad was and couldn't stop chattering.

My husband thoroughly enjoyed his Father's Day and it didn't cost him any fuel. Best of all, he gave three other Dads the best gift ever – touring Niagara in a single-engine Cessna!

Life Lesson from the Chair: Whatever your passion; it is best shared with others.

Until next haircut...

Alice: The Force Seems to Be With Her

Alice is one of *those* people. You know, the lucky kind who are always entering contests on the radio or internet? And often winning! She seems to attract abundance into her life so easily.

She and her husband love to travel. They go away three or four times a year. One time, in the Bahamas, she won $3000.00 playing the slots. She put it aside, thinking, "There's another trip!"

I remember one time when Alice arrived for highlights. She walked into my salon with a big grin on her face and casually mentioned how she'd won $10,000 in the lottery the week before.

"That's awesome! You must be so excited!" I told her. "What are you going to do with that money?"

She and her husband planned to take some more trips. But first, she had to drive to Toronto to collect her winnings. "I love to travel, but I hate driving to Toronto!" she told me. "Too much traffic and confusion. The Lottery Corp said I could send my ticket via registered mail and they'd send me a cheque."

I thought, "Boy! I wouldn't put a winning ticket in the mail even if I did register it. I'd drive to Toronto in a heartbeat for $10,000!" But, Alice said it was no big deal. "I've had a good week," she explained. "Three days ago, I won $1000.00 on the radio!"

I just shook my head in disbelief. This woman attracts more things!

From the Hairdresser's Chair

As I was doing her highlights, she told me another story. Before coming to her appointment, she had stopped at Sears to pay her account. She noticed a sign advertising a free DVD player if you booked a trip that week.

"I marched right in and told them my husband and I had booked our trip three weeks ago. If I'd known, we would have held off booking until now!"

The travel agent asked her to wait and she'd see what she could do. A few minutes later, she returned and told Alice, "You've booked so many trips through us, I've managed to pull some strings and give you the DVD player!"

Alice said, "It's in the back seat of my car right now."

Finishing her hair, I thought, "Wow! This woman has had such an incredible streak of luck lately". As she went to pay me, I saw the winning lottery ticket in her wallet, still waiting to be mailed.

No wonder she'd been so lucky! Carrying that winning ticket around gave her very strong feelings of abundance. Every time she opened her purse and saw the ticket, she just knew...money is coming!

Life Lesson from the Chair: Money is like everything else in our universe. It's just a form of energy our thoughts can make real for us.

Until next haircut...

PART TWO

Kris Hits a Home Run with Sarah

Susan is a regular client of mine. Her daughter, Sarah, has long hair and only comes in about once a year for subtle highlights. Still, I hear all about Sarah from her mother and have come to know her over the years.

Sarah had dated Kris for a few years in her early 20s, then the relationship ended and they both moved on. Five years later, though, they hooked up again. Both had matured and realized that they were meant to be together.

A couple of years passed, with Sarah patiently waiting to get engaged. Acting in plays is one of her hobbies and she loves attention. Kris knew any proposal had better be big!

Shopping for the perfect ring, Sarah found exactly what she wanted. It was unusual, unique − a diamond and sapphire ring. The woman selling it told her that she'd once been engaged to a man from Dubai, which is where the ring had come from.

But after he returned to Dubai for work, she received a break-up letter from him and never saw him again. After a few years, she met and married someone else, so she decided the time was right to sell this ring.

Sarah had found the woman online. She and Kris met at a local jeweler to have the ring appraised and set a fair price both agreed on. Sarah knew Kris had purchased the ring, but she had no idea when he might propose.

Time passed. She was ready for her ring! However, Kris had some big plans.

Every year, the church congregation that Sarah and her mother Susan, belonged to, would go to Toronto to catch a Blue Jays baseball game. So far, about 130 people from their church had purchased tickets. Kris and Sarah loved to go watch the Jays play.

Kris asked Susan for permission to marry Sarah and confided that he planned to pop the question at the game, with the help of the large group from their church. The more the merrier and the bigger the experience for Sarah. Kris knew his future bride so well!

Even the priest who would eventually perform the marriage ceremony would be at the ball game! So Susan and her future son-in-law planned the surprise engagement.

Kris' sister, Steffany, made signs on five sheets of laminated banquet table paper. One side read "Sarah, I love you. Will you marry me?" The other side said, "Our Lady of the Scapular Church Loves the Blue Jays!" This made it easy for them to get their props in order.

They checked with the Rogers Centre to see if Kris' proposal could be shown on the Jumbo Tron; unfortunately, this could no longer be certain. They'd just have to hope that the rows of people with the huge signage would be picked up. Susan kept her fingers crossed!

When game day finally came, Sarah said to her mom, "I'm not sure if we can make it tonight. I'm tired. I've had a long day at work." Susan stayed calm and said, "That's fine. I'll see you on Sunday at church".

Her mom thought Sarah might be testing her to see her reaction. Susan just played it cool; she knew Kris would get her there.

Sure enough, they arrived at the Rogers Centre. Kris and Sarah were sitting in the first row of seats in their section with the church group all seated behind them. Susan sat directly behind Sarah; several members of both families were in the seats around them and the priest sat a few rows behind Sarah.

In the middle of the 5th inning, Kris planned to propose. The group behind them held all the signs "Our Lady of the Scapular Church Loves the Blue Jays!" Kris had instructed them to flip them over at this break.

When the time came, Kris tapped Sarah's shoulder to turn around. The church group had just flipped over the signs! Sarah saw the message, "I love you, Sarah. Will you marry me?" She quickly turned back around and there was Kris, down on one knee with her beautiful ring in hand.

Her mouth dropped open and then she screamed with excitement. "Yes, yes, YES!"

The priest was right there, on hand to bless the ring, as Kris slipped it on Sarah's finger. The Jumbo Tron caught them on camera just as they kissed and flashed their big moment on the big screen for the whole stadium to see!

Sarah was overjoyed with her engagement! They set the wedding date for July.

Life Lesson from the Chair: *Patience truly is a virtue – one that is becoming more and more rare, in our fast-paced digital world.*

Until next haircut...

Belinda and Don's Plan for Living Large - and Long!

Have you ever thought about what you're going to be like at age 80? Most of us plan for the financial side of retirement, but what about our health?

Belinda is a client of mine who's originally from Colorado. She and her husband, Don – a retired doctor in Ontario, had both been widowed when they met through a distant relative at a family reunion. When they married, Belinda decided to keep her home in Colorado and spend time there every winter.

One Christmas, she came in for a hair appointment. Snow was falling, and we chatted about all the high-calorie foods that tempted us this time of year.

I mentioned how much I enjoyed my aunt's delicious baked brie. She takes a wheel of brie, adds brown sugar, pecans, raisins, butter and wraps it up in a sheet of puff pastry. Yum! My mouth was watering just talking about it.

Belinda said, "I love brie, too. It's my favourite cheese and there's some left over in my fridge at home right now. But it's dangerous. I can't keep my fingers out of it! It's so fattening. Too much is bad for my cholesterol."

I suggested that she get her husband to help her finish the cheese. "Oh, Don won't eat brie, or any other cheese."

"Doesn't he like it?" I asked.

"That's the trouble," she said. "He absolutely loves it! But, about fifteen years ago, he had a heart scare. Ever since then, he has really taken good care of himself. He chooses healthy foods, learns even more about what's good for him and exercises regularly. Before his heart scare, he was over-worked, had poor eating habits, low energy – that health scare really woke him up."

I wondered, "Hmmm. Do we really need a scare to get healthy?" and decided that yes! Some people do.

Our conversation turned to what Belinda and Don do all winter in Colorado. They stayed very active because they both loved to ski. Belinda skied about three times a week, but Don hooked up with a group of men and they hit the slopes every day! He really does have a lot of energy.

I asked Belinda when they would be coming back to Ontario. She said it would be earlier than usual that year. They would normally stay in Colorado until the end of May, but this year, Don would be celebrating his 80th birthday in March. His family planned to have a big party for him.

"Wow!" I said. "Eighty years old and skiing every day. I think I'll pass on my aunt's baked brie appetizer this Christmas!"

It really makes you think, doesn't it? Where do you want to be when you are 80? What do you want to be doing?

Life Lesson from the Chair: *An Egyptian proverb says, "Health is a crown on a well man's head that only a sick man can see." We take our health for granted until we no longer have it. We need to invest in our health and well-being now, no matter what our age, if we're to see a healthy return later in life.*

Until next haircut…

Joyce Knows She's Never Alone

"Opening yourself up to the gifts of God means trusting that He loves you and will provide for you." Joyce mentions this almost every hair appointment.

I enjoy hearing her comments about her strong faith. She lives a life of gratitude and appreciation, always so thankful for all the little blessings that come her way.

She said with such a knowing that the act of trust, or faith, is how we join ourselves to the source of what we need. She was absolutely right, and that Tuesday night, her belief was to be tested.

Joyce lived in an apartment in Fort Erie. It was only 20 minutes away from her job across the river in Buffalo, New York via the I-90. That day, it had been snowing and blowing for hours. Everyone was talking about the bad weather.

Joyce finished her shift and was relieved to see her gas gauge was almost at full when she headed into the storm to drive home. As she got on the Interstate, she recalled the Blizzard of '77 (aka White Death although, miraculously, no one had actually died).

That storm had shut down Buffalo, Fort Erie and the surrounding areas for five days. Although she had been home then, so many people had been stranded all over. Even in their vehicles.

I remembered that storm, too. I had taken two clients home with me. Along with a few other people who had been stranded, we were together for three days. My younger brother and sister had slept at their school for two nights.

Joyce told me that the winter storm was slowing up all the trucks on the I-90, however she felt safe staying behind a big transport. He was guiding her along the snow-covered highway. She just kept focusing on his taillights; otherwise, she couldn't see a thing through the snow squalls.

She said, "All of a sudden, all the traffic came to a stop. I could barely see out my window, but I knew there were two transport trucks, one in front and one behind me. It was midnight; I had been on the road for 45 minutes."

Nothing was moving. Joyce was too nervous to get out and ask other drivers what was going on. Instead, she started to pray and she felt her fear melt away. She just knew she would be okay and was thankful she had lots of gas.

Her cell phone was charged and she had lots of minutes, yet she didn't want to call anyone and worry them. What could her grown children do, anyway? She kept praying, feeling calm and at peace.

After a couple of hours, she could feel the call of nature. Looking around the car for a solution, she found an empty Tim Horton's coffee cup. "Perfect!" she chuckled.

She locked the car doors for privacy, as if someone might be wandering by, then wiggled her pants down and balanced the cup to find ultimate relief. Putting the full cup on the floor in front of the empty passenger seat, she pulled herself together again, without a spill.

Joyce said, "The things you can do when you have to! I was so careful in opening the car door so I could dump the piddle without spilling a drop and save the empty cup for next time! Thank you, Timmy's!"

Three hours passed. She turned her car off to save gas, until it got so cold she needed to warm up again. She kept the window open a crack and just kept praying.

"All of a sudden, someone tapped on my window," she said. "A policeman! He wanted to make sure I was okay. He asked if I had enough gas and told me I should shut the car off every so often. He said they were doing all they could, but the plows were having trouble getting to the highway to clear it."

She knew it was going to be a long night. Joyce prayed again, asking for protection for everyone and to keep her safe, warm and comfortable. Looking through the car, she found the owner's manual and a book of short stories to read.

I said, "Thank you! Out loud for keeping me occupied!" she exclaimed. "I smiled inside and had a knowing. I just got comfortable and knew I wasn't alone, no matter how long it took to get moving again."

She kept praying.

Four hours went by. Nothing was moving. Joyce drifted off to sleep a few times and had to answer nature's call again, but she had learned to handle that pretty well!

"Those hours felt like days. At 8:00 am, the sun was up and I was feeling hungry and thirsty. Finally, another policeman arrived to say that traffic would be moving shortly. I looked at my fuel gauge and thought I'd be fine for a while yet. I was glad my car's just a little 4-cylinder!"

The traffic started to move. "Yippee! I'm finally going to get home!"

As Joyce crossed the Peace Bridge, she felt so relieved after having been stranded on the highway all night. "When I got into my apartment and phoned work to say I wouldn't be in after having sat on the I-90 for ten hours, my boss told me to have a good sleep – I deserved a day off!"

From the Hairdresser's Chair

She jumped into a nice, hot bath, made herself a cup of tea then went to bed. She said her covers had never felt so good. When she awoke, she phoned her family to let them know what had happened and that she was fine.

Full of gratitude for being home safe, with a tear running down her cheek, she prayed again.

Life Lesson from the Chair: *Witnessing the faith that others place in God strengthens our own.*

Until next haircut…

Jeremy: Boys and Their Toys

One fall day, Jeremy sat in my chair for his monthly haircut and told me he was thinking about buying a motorcycle. It just so happened that my husband was selling one of his.

I hesitated a bit, but then I told him and Jeremy asked to see it after his haircut. His eyes lit up when we walked into the garage and he saw Dave's Kawasaki 1500 cc motorcycle.

"I love the look of this bike! It's my favourite colour, too!"

I told him to go ahead and sit on it. He loved the feel of the bike. After every haircut, he'd check on the bike and say how tempting it was for him to buy it. By January, he did.

Jeremy's wife, Nicole, is a client of mine, too. When she told me that she'd been using a wrench to start her washing machine for years and that her dryer was on the fritz, I started to feel guilty about Jeremy having bought the motorcycle from my husband.

"Oh, I'm fine with Jeremy's purchase," she assured me. "You know my husband with his toys."

"What IS it with boys and their toys?" I asked. My husband was selling *one* of his motorcycles. And he owned a small plane. Jeremy already had a boat, a Sea-do and a snowmobile. And Nicole starts her laundry by whacking the washer with a wrench?!!

From the Hairdresser's Chair

"You're not disappointed that I showed Jeremy Dave's bike, are you?" I asked her.

"Oh, no. He would have bought one anyway. There's a sign in his office that says, 'He who dies with the most toys, wins'!" We both chuckled. These men – they think WE spend too much!

A few weeks later, Jeremy arrived for his monthly haircut. With a cast on his arm! He had broken his wrist during his motorcycle lesson. "Oh, Jeremy. I feel so responsible for this," I told him.

"Don't be silly. It's my fault. I hit the front brake too hard." Jeremy smiled and said, "I'm ready to get back on the bike once this cast comes off."

I was sure he'd heal quickly because he was so fit and determined, but his physio went on all summer. It was fall again before he was back to normal. No motorcycle this year.

When Jeremy came in for his October appointment, he said, "You won't believe it, but I sold the motorcycle!" It made me wonder. Do these boys really need their toys? Hmm…does this mean Nicole will finally get a new washer and dryer?!!

Life Lesson from the Chair: Be very careful what you ask for. You just might get more than you bargained for!

Until next haircut…

Barb's Trip and Triplets

Barb sat in my chair, so excited about her upcoming 2-week trip to Italy and a Mediterranean cruise. But, it wasn't just the trip she was excited about.

Two years before, her niece, Mary, had been an egg donor for Dominic and his partner, a gay couple from Italy. Mary had provided seven eggs, however, the in vitro fertilization hadn't worked. At that point, Dominic decided to fly to Ontario and meet Mary.

The two discovered they were both aestheticians. Dominic and his partner owned a salon and spa in Rome. They became instant friends and adored each other.

Soon, it was time to try the procedure again. Mary provided three more eggs, they were fertilized in vitro and implanted into a surrogate mother named Donna, in the hope that at least one embryo would grow to maturity.

This time, all went well. Dominic is the natural father, Mary is the biological mother and Donna was carrying the baby.

During Donna's first ultrasound, they discovered that there were actually three babies! They were surprised and delighted, knowing in advance that this could happen. Dominic and his partner were overjoyed and busy preparing for the arrival of triplets, who were eventually born in a hospital in Hamilton, Ontario because in vitro/surrogacy birth is not available in Italy.

Dominic, his mother and an aunt arrived for the birth and to take the three baby girls back to Italy. The girls were now 13 months old and the real reason Barb was so excited about her trip!

The men were ecstatic that some of their baby girls' relatives were coming to visit! They had kept the Ontario branch of the family up to date on the triplets' progress through email and photos. Mary – the egg donor – enjoyed watching the girls grow into active toddlers. She had a soft spot in her heart for Dominic. He'd become like a brother to her.

Barb and her sister would be the first relatives to meet the triplets since they were moved home to Italy. At last the day came for them to go. They were to meet the girls the second day they were there, before going on their Mediterranean cruise.

Barb said she felt like she was going out on a first date that morning, when they drove to Dominic's home. "What will they think of me? How do I look? What do I say?"

She knew there would be some language barrier even though her niece, Mary, hadn't had a problem understanding Dominic when he visited Canada.

Her stomach was churning as they pulled into the driveway. It was a beautiful and modest home, rather small, but stunning. Arriving at the front door, they were welcomed in by Dominic. Lots of hugs were exchanged and then he escorted them downstairs to a large playroom where the three girls – Juliet, Abigail and Alexandra - were sitting, playing in a circle.

The tears rolled down Barb's cheeks as she took in these three little miracles sitting in front of her. One looked just like her niece, Mary, had when she was a baby.

When Dominic handed Barb one of the babies to hold, she started to cry. Then all three of them were crying! Of course, Barb was a stranger to them. The nanny came in, settled them down and said it would soon be time for their nap.

They watched as the nanny got them ready for nap time. She was wonderful with the girls and you could tell she was experienced. She'd been with them from Day One, five days a week, from 10:00 am until 6:00 pm. Barb and her sister kissed all the little ones on the forehead.

Barb thought, "Thank goodness for the extra help!" They all headed up to the kitchen. It was beautiful, decorated in red and white. They relaxed at the table with coffee and cookies.

From the Hairdresser's Chair

Dominic was so happy to meet them and regretted that his partner couldn't be there, but someone had to stay and work at the salon.

Soon, Dominic would be going back to work, too. They had found daycare for the girls, right next to their home. The nanny would also stay on part-time. With triplets, they'll need all the help they can get! Dominic and his partner felt blessed to have family close by, too. Both their nonas and aunties were a big help during that first year.

The babies only slept 15 minutes before they were ready to play again. "Not much rest in this house!" Barb thought. She and her sister gave Dominic a gift from Canada: three little t-shirts with "Canada" across the front. He was so pleased.

He surprised them with a gift of his own – a chance to visit the salon and spa for some pampering. They thanked him, but declined because they had already made other plans.

"You turned down a spa in Rome?" I teased her.

The two Canadian visitors said their good-byes with a few tears all around, then headed back to their hotel. They thoroughly enjoyed their cruise, all the sights, and other entertainments on their trip. When they returned home, though, no one wanted to hear about those things. They were just anxious to hear about their visit with the triplets!

Barb had brought home many pictures of the girls to share with her niece. She told Mary what a great father Dominic was; he just loves his three girls. Barb decided to visit her parents, who would be the triplets' great-grandparents. She wasn't sure how they felt about the triplets.

To Barb's surprise, her 89-year-old father had already posted pictures of his triplet grandchildren on Facebook! He was so proud! He wanted to know everything.

Dominic and his partner hope to marry someday. Same-sex marriage is not recognized yet in Italy. Who knows? Maybe they'll be back in Ontario for a wedding!

Life Lesson from the Chair: *Every child is a precious gift and a blessing to be loved and cherished no matter how the little one arrived, where or to whom.*

Until next haircut…

Kathy Demands Respect

Every year, Kathy enjoys volunteering her time to the air show that comes to her city. The event draws thousands of people, and extra help is needed with parking for the handicapped.

Kathy's task was to take wheelchair customers and any seniors in need of assistance to a preferred parking area. Golf carts would then transport them to the stands to watch the show.

Most of the seniors she served were very appreciative of her help. Except for one older man in his eighties.

He had his own scooter on the back of his truck and refused to pay the $5 entrance fee (already half off the regular price of admission). He was cranky. He swore at Kathy. He griped that he had no money and, because the government owed him, he should get in for free.

Then he sped off to park in the preferred area. His attitude stunned Kathy, but she didn't think it was fair to let it go. She thought, "You can't go to the corner store for milk and then say you're not going to pay for it because the government owes you!"

She radioed her husband at the parking area entrance to tell him about the incident. He just happened to be standing by a police officer who was directing traffic. The officer overheard the complaint on the walkie-talkie, then hopped on a golf cart to confront the snarky senior.

As you can imagine, it caused a stir. People were watching to see what was going on. At first, the elderly man was nasty with the officer. He obviously had a chip on his shoulder about something.

The officer handled it very well. Kathy was starting to feel bad for having complained, as she heard the officer set the old codger straight.

Still, it wasn't the $5. It was the principle. If the senior had told Kathy he'd like to see the show closer than from the side of the road but he couldn't afford the fee, she'd have gladly paid his way. If only he'd shown her that respect.

Not long after, as Kathy was busy helping other seniors to park, she felt a tap on her shoulder. It was the cranky senior! He apologized for his earlier behavior, then handed her a $50.00 bill to pay his way.

She accepted his apology and thanked him for paying. Then she knew she'd made the right decision in lodging her protest. He hadn't weaseled out of paying and he'd learned a valuable lesson. The man was truly sorry for the way he had acted.

Life Lesson from the Chair: A positive attitude and goodwill toward others will always lift you higher. A negative attitude will drag you, and them, to the ground. Don't let negative emotions cause your reputation to crash and burn.

Until next haircut…

Lorraine Just Zips It!

Adventure does not exactly top my client, Lorraine's, list. At least, not until she and her husband went to visit their son, Joe, in Saskatchewan.

Joe wanted his Dad to go zip-lining with him. He agreed, but, when Lorraine piped up and said she'd go, too – he just laughed. "You can't do that. You have a bad knee! Joe and I will go. You can just wait at the picnic table, read a book and relax while you wait for us." (He must have been remembering her one hundred attempts to snow ski).

Lorraine commented to me, "Suddenly, adventure popped right up to the top of my list!" She told her husband and son, "Oh, yes I can! I feel good, I'm healthy and I've been exercising."

Then she began to think, "Oh my. He's right. I don't have very good knees. And I'm not very strong." But, I was determined that I could do this!

Arriving at Cypress Park at noon, they went to the office to sign up and pay their admission fee only to learn that the next available group wouldn't go out until 5:00 pm.

There were only three spots left and they had to wait. Dave and Joe signed up. Lorraine hesitated. "I'll just watch the group that's heading out now before I commit," she thought.

She walked over to where they started, took one look and said there's no way. A 50-foot rope ladder went straight up to a small platform. "Where's the elevator up?" she wondered.

She was terrified! But she told herself, "Just do it, Lorraine!" She walked over and signed up. Now she had five whole hours to think about it. The three of them hung around the park and went on a short hike to kill time. Finally, it was 4:30. Time to go get prepped.

Lorraine thought she might throw up. Had she mentioned she was also afraid of heights?

A young fellow gave them their briefing. There were five other people – a family with two teenagers and a little boy of about eight.

Everyone was shown how to harness up, issued helmets, and then given a detailed explanation of what they were going to do. There were seven platforms with a telephone pole on the fourth, which they would be climbing.

Lorraine watched in horror as the first few climbed up the ladder. It was swinging in the breeze. Her poor husband was nervous for her!

They climbed up in pairs. Lorraine and her husband started up together. She said, "We had to stay in sync. And I kept wanting to hog the middle of the ladder!"

Mouth dry, heart pounding, she knew she had to keep going and she never looked down.

Reaching the top, she pulled herself up. There were now eight of them perched on this tiny platform blowing in the wind. There was a tree in the centre. The eight-year-old was clinging to it. Lorraine went over and told the boy, "Hey! Make room for me!" Then she clung to the tree, too, completely terrified!

"Zip-lining has to be easier than this," she thought, and off she went.

She landed backwards, so they had to drag her up the slope to the platform backwards. But, she made it. "Two more zips and then the phone pole." she told herself. "I'm just going to get off here, I've had enough!"

She landed on the fourth platform and they were still 30 feet in the air with no way down. She had to go up. With no way out of it, she told herself again, "Just DO it!"

Lorraine climbed 30 more feet up the telephone pole. It was much harder than going up the rope ladder, and she just kept repeating that Nike slogan: "Just DO it!!!"

Four more zips and this dreadful misadventure would be over. Now, she was starting to get the hang of it and was finally landing the right way.

She reached the last zip, at last relaxed enough to enjoy it. She landed, feeling totally exhilarated.

"Wow!" I said to her. "You really stepped out of your comfort zone in a big way!"

She agreed but said, "Yeah. I'll never, EVER do it again, but it was worth it!"

Life Lesson from the Chair: *You'll never know what you can do until you try. Just when you think you've reached your limits, they'll expand to reveal yet another possibility.*

Until next haircut...

From the Hairdresser's Chair

Sharon Turns a Problem – and Herself - Around

Sharon has four sons, but no daughter. She hoped that, one day, she'd have four daughters-in-law she would adore. Unfortunately, things weren't going well with her first son's wife.

"They live about three hours away, so we don't visit often," she told me. "We usually have them overnight or we'll stay at their house. My daughter-in-law just never seems to warm up to me," she said, all teary and sad.

"I just don't know what to do. I go out of my way to make her feel comfortable when they visit us. I take lots of homemade food when we visit them. My husband and I offer to babysit. But, she just seems to brush me off, as if I'm not important to her."

Every year, Sharon would make a special day or even a weekend with each of her sons. They all looked forward to it. She'd ask what they wanted to do. It might be going out for dinner and to the theatre in downtown Toronto.

Her younger son loves Nascar, so one year they went to Michigan for a Nascar Race.

Sharon couldn't figure out the problem with her daughter-in-law. Could she be jealous of her relationship with her son?

"Now they have twin boys who are four and a daughter, who's turning six. My husband and I will babysit on occasion, so they can have a weekend getaway. For some reason, my daughter-in-law never seems to appreciate it."

When I told Sharon that you can't change other people; you can only change the way you react to their behaviour, she said, "That's hard to do."

"For instance, they invited us up for the weekend and we were going to babysit on the Saturday evening. When we arrived, my daughter-in-law ran out the door in her workout clothes and said, 'I'm off to the gym! Find something to make for dinner and I'll see you later.' She just flattens me. I feel unworthy of her attention."

"You need to look for something you like and appreciate about her," I suggested.

She said, "That's really hard to do."

"Well," I continued, "is she a great Mom to your three grandchildren? Is she a wonderful wife to your son?"

"Yes," Sharon replied.

"Then focus on that. Here's an exercise you can do.

From the Hairdresser's Chair

Take out a picture of her and a piece of paper. Write down three things you're most grateful for about her. Look at the picture and say out loud 'I am so grateful (use her name) to you for (fill in the blank).' Go through each one and give thanks at the end by saying, 'Thank you, thank you, THANK you.' You'll probably have tears. Believe me, this is a powerful exercise. Just remember that you can only change yourself."

"Hmmm…I'll try," she replied.

A few months passed. Then Sharon came in to see me. "I do your exercise often," she said, "and our relationship has really improved! We went to visit them recently and I decided to tell both my son and my daughter-in-law that my husband and I thought they were amazing parents to our grandchildren."

"I told them it gave us such peace seeing how they care for their children and that we appreciated the love, nurturing and guidance they've committed to raising them."

Sharon's daughter-in-law was so pleased, she gave her a huge hug and said, "Thank you!" Something had changed in that moment.

The next month, her daughter-in-law invited Sharon to attend an event with her and her own mother. When she arrived, she offered her a cup of tea, then sat down and they had a lovely chat.

She also told Sharon how much she appreciated her watching her kids. None of that had ever happened before!

Sharon has completely changed the way she feels about her daughter-in-law, and as a result, everything else has changed. Sharon is so pleased to have found the closeness she had longed for all these years.

Life Lesson from the Chair: *People spend a lot less time thinking about us than we fear they do. Being kind to them first gives them the chance they may have been waiting for to reciprocate.*

Until next haircut…

Neil Grows Up and into his Higher Purpose

Neil was an extremely shy boy. Whenever his Dad, Chris, brought him for a haircut, I could barely get him to talk. My questions would get a one-word answer.

"How's school, Neil?"

"Fine."

"What's your favourite subject?"

"History."

"What's so interesting about history?"

"The teacher!"

That was pretty much it. Neil wore glasses and liked to hide behind his longish hair. He wanted me to leave his bangs extremely long over the frames of his eyeglasses and he liked his hair to touch his shoulders.

I always did exactly as he asked. That way, I hoped he would learn to trust me and keep coming back for a trim.

Chris encouraged him to go for a shorter cut, but Neil wouldn't do it. He needed to hide behind his hair and glasses.

Years went by and Neil would still only have a trim! His shyness stayed the same. When he finally reached high school, in Grade 11, he got a job at the border. He worked in the ticket booth, collecting money as drivers came through on their way back from a visit to the States.

It was the perfect first job for Neil because each car would only stop briefly to pay at the window and he didn't have to talk much at all. Still, it would help him come out of his shell little by little.

He started letting me cut a bit more hair off and you could actually see his gorgeous eyes and beautiful long eyelashes! We started to have more conversations and I noticed a nice young man starting to emerge.

When Neil graduated from high school, he moved away to go to university. This was his choice and his Dad knew it was the right decision.

Being on his own and living in another city would allow him to search out his purpose, gain confidence in himself, and maybe even learn to be a little bold.

Chris was a regular client, so I'd see him often and we'd talk about Neil. Chris told me he was so proud of his son and that he was doing very well in university.

From the Hairdresser's Chair

He'd made a few friends and was a pet student of his professors. Neil graduated with a four-year bachelor's degree in his favourite subject from the start. History!

His Dad was beaming as he shared this with me. Neil decided to keep going and study another year, walking away with his Master's degree.

That shy, sweet boy had discovered his passion for teaching. Neil announced his plans to study and work in Korea. He had found the nerve to go into unexplored territory and was brave enough to live his life creatively.

Chris flew over the first year and had an amazing time with his son. He was proud of the man Neil had become! He worked in Korea for two years and has now moved to Scotland, where he is back in school going for his PhD. He found the courage to follow his heart and his intuition.

His Dad was just in for a haircut. It had been a while since we'd spoken of Neil. "Has he finished school now?" I asked.

Chris smiled with an eager look to share this special news. "Neil is close to finishing and has been speaking at many universities, including Glasgow, Birmingham, and he was recently giving a presentation at the University of Stockholm in Sweden!"

My mouth dropped open. This shy little boy has certainly come a very long way. He now has a short, clean-cut haircut, speaks at universities and will receive his PhD in 2016. It took Neil a while, but he has found his purpose now.

Life Lesson from the Chair: *Our world tends to be run by extroverts, but studies show that introverts make better leaders because they prefer to listen rather than speak. Watch out for the quiet ones, indeed!*

Until next haircut…

Tom and Ellie Took Baby Steps to a Better Life

Tom and his late wife, Ellie, were clients and friends of mine from 'way back. We met at the daycare when our children were two years old.

I'd been invited to do a little "hairdressing hour". I braided the little girls' hair, put some gel in the boys' to make it spiky. The kids had a lot of fun. I just wanted them to feel comfortable about going for their haircuts.

After that, Ellie brought her daughter, Kerrie to my salon for a haircut and the rest, as they say, is history. Because now Kerrie is 34 years old!

Over the years, I enjoyed doing hair for Ellie, Tom and both their daughters. There were the usual special events, like Grade 8 graduations, high school proms and university graduations. But the most exciting was when Kerrie got engaged and planned to be married in Cuba.

My husband, Dave, and I were invited to go! It didn't take much to persuade Dave because he'd known Tom and Ellie for a long time, too.

Kerrie was delighted to have us attend. I did the hair for her and the whole wedding party. Of the 26 wedding guests, I knew at least half of them as clients.

103

Two years later, Kerrie and her husband were blessed with the arrival of a beautiful baby girl. They named her Adelaide. Tom and Ellie were very proud grandparents!

A few months after her birth, the family noticed that Addy didn't make eye contact and couldn't hold her head up. At first, they thought it was normal because all babies progress at different rates. Addy was born in September.

By January, they decided something was wrong. They needed to have her checked. The doctors agreed this wee one was not developing properly.

Many tests later, they discovered she'd been born with a very rare birth defect. They also felt little Addy would be blind. Everyone was devastated. How could this be? Kerrie had done everything right during her pregnancy. The odds were a million to one.

The tests continued. The results and prognoses grew worse. Addy started having seizures. Kerrie and her family were beating a steady path to the Emergency Room door.

Finally, after many visits to the hospital and to specialists, Addy's condition stabilized a bit and they were able to keep it somewhat under control.

At first, the family was in denial and kept hoping a new doctor would come up with a better outcome for Addy. But they finally accepted there was no hope for their beautiful baby girl to have a normal life.

Many tears flowed until they pulled themselves together and asked for strength, guidance and courage.

By marshalling these inner resources, they managed to create a life for Addy on her terms. One that was full of love, compassion and acceptance.

One day, Tom and Ellie turned up at my hair salon with a new sense of freedom from the pain they'd been suffering over Addy's future. After having experienced so many sad visits with them, this was a very welcome change.

They'd finally moved beyond their pain, to a place where they felt truly blessed to have Addy in their lives. They enjoyed her smiles and soft giggles when they walked into her room. They found their joy in making Addy happy. She taught them how to be loving and kind. To forgive.

I never saw judgment in them. Addy had shown them a new and different, better way of looking at life.

Life Lesson from the Chair: Sometimes, the smallest creatures make the greatest teachers.

Until next haircut…

Jane's Visualization Victory

Jane is a client of mine who studies the Law of Attraction and always puts into practice everything she learns about it. Here's just one amazing example among many.

There was a radio contest that chose 75 people from all who entered. Each would be given a key, but only one of the keys would start the new car the station was giving away.

Of course, Jane was selected as one of those 75! Now she knew that her odds of winning were good: 1 in 75. (Our chances of winning a lottery are one in more than a million).

Right away, Jane started with her Law of Attraction techniques. She drove by the dealership every day and visualized herself in that car. She told everyone she was going to get a new vehicle. She convinced herself that *her* key would turn that car on!

She and her husband even went as far as taking the exact vehicle, same colour, out for a test drive. They drove it all over, experiencing how it would feel to own such a car.

As her husband pulled into the dealership, Jane suddenly said, "Wait! I forgot something. I need to start the car and feel it in my body as the engine is turning over."

From the Hairdresser's Chair

She jumped into the driver's seat, closed her eyes and turned the key. She felt the ignition and allowed the feeling of the engine to rumble through her body.

She just sat there for a few moments, her hand on the key, feeling the engine purr. Then she looked at her husband and said, "Okay. We're done!" and off they went.

He looked at her strangely. "Was all that really necessary?" he asked. "Yes!" Jane replied. "I know what I'm doing!"

Jane was to be at the radio station in a few days to pick up her key. When she went to bed at night, she visualized herself sitting in the car, turning the key and feeling the engine start.

When she picked up her key the day of the draw, she had an absolute knowing it was the right key. She was number 42 to test her key.

She patiently watched while all the people were trying to start the vehicle with no luck. Number 40 tried and failed. Then number 41. It was Jane's turn next.

She sat in the car, closed her eyes and turned the key. The car started!

Isn't that a great story? I love it!

I know that visualization is the key to attracting what you want. I've often used it myself with amazing results. Here's one story that comes to mind.

At the end of my 3-day motorcycle training course, I failed my test because I went too fast. I only allowed myself to be disappointed for 30 seconds. I parked my bike and made an appointment to retake my test in three weeks.

I went home and told everyone what a great weekend I'd had. I had learned so much. If anyone said, "Aw, it's too bad you failed." I'd just tell them how much fun I'd had and how I'd loved the experience.

I knew I had to start visualizing, so I created a movie in my mind. I pictured myself doing all nine tests and completing them exactly how I should. I did this all day long and I also practiced every day at the school parking lot in our neighbourhood.

I decided to add a little extra visualizing. In my mind's eye, I saw myself in my car picking up my cell phone and calling my husband, asking him to break out the champagne!

Each time I did this, goose bumps, rushes and shivers would run through my body. The more I felt this, the more I believed it. I kept rehearsing it over and over again.

From the Hairdresser's Chair

The day finally came. I was nervous, but ready. Just before I got out of my car, I placed my cell phone in the exact spot where I had seen it in my mind.

I took my test and you already know what happened. Of course I passed it this time! The women who had failed, told me how they had beaten themselves up after their first attempt. They walked in with negative comments. I heard things like, "Oh, I'll probably fail again!"

When I received my paperwork, I headed to my car and saw the phone sitting there, waiting for me. I picked it up and made the call I'd been picturing for weeks. "Break out the champagne!"

We didn't even have any, but that's what I had rehearsed so that's exactly what I said. When I got home, my husband opened a bottle of wine and we celebrated!

Life Lesson from the Chair: Three simple words will help you achieve whatever your heart and mind desire: Conceive, believe, and receive. Visualization is the tool that gets things started and moves you along to the desired result.

Until next haircut...

Crystal Has the Best Day of Her Life

Ever since she was a little girl, Crystal had dreamt of her wedding day. She had always pictured her wavy, waist-length hair in beautiful curls topped with a tiara and floor-length veil.

She started dating early, falling in love at 17. But there was no engagement ring. At 19, she had a beautiful daughter. Still no engagement ring. In fact, the relationship itself ended.

A few years later, she fell in love again and had a son. No ring. No wedding. No relationship. There she was, a single mom with two children still dreaming of her wedding day. Crystal focused on bringing her children up as best she could.

She loved being a mom! She decided to open a daycare at her home. At the time, she only had enough room for four children, but she loved the idea of working from home, to be there for her own kids.

It wasn't too long before she met an Italian man, six years older than she was. He'd never married and he had no children. Crystal really liked him, and in no time, they were a couple.

He was very good to her and her children. The "instant family" suited him well. Once again, she was head over heels in love. But no ring. No wedding plans.

From the Hairdresser's Chair

Eventually, Crystal and Vince moved in together and bought a house. He was a great stepdad to her children and they had a beautiful home together.

They moved the daycare in. There was plenty of room now. Crystal created a nap room with eight small cots, a playroom and an eating area. She could take on 8 to 10 children.

For safety, they fenced in the backyard, and for fun, they added a playground with a swing and slide. In no time, the house was efficient and running well for her business. Life seemed like it couldn't get any better. Crystal was very happy, except for one thing. Still no wedding!

She would often chat with me about how she would like her hair on her wedding day. She would visit the salon every couple months for highlights on her waist-length hair. (A big job for me!)

Even though she lived only four houses away, Crystal always drove to her appointment. We often joked about it. She'd laugh and say, "It might rain!" My husband would tease her about it, too. Sometimes I'd think she drove just to get a rise out of Dave!

One day, it happened. Crystal showed up for her appointment with an engagement ring! She was ecstatic with joy and spent about eight months planning her wedding. She often joked that she'd waited twelve years for her ring and the big day.

She knew exactly what she wanted, and of course, there were many practices on her long hair prior to the wedding.

All the details were in place: bridesmaids, venue, and dinner – Crystal even bought a little bridal dress and veil for her tiny dog, Bella. (Bella was all of about 4 pounds). She was to walk down the aisle in her wee dress.

Tiny red roses ran down the leash. Crystal's teenage daughter was the bridesmaid who was to walk Bella down the aisle. It was important to Crystal to have her pet there, too. Bella was family!

The day before the wedding, a big heat wave caused a power outage in most parts of the city. All I could think about was Crystal, being in a panic; no hydro and not knowing when it will be back up and running.

But this didn't discourage her. Crystal was at the hall with flashlights, decorating. She was getting married the next day no matter what!

I quickly made plans for an alternative place to do her hair in case we still had no power. Her hair simply had to be perfect! Luckily, the power was back by morning and plans stayed the same. Whew!

For me, the highlight of this story happened on the morning of her big day.

From the Hairdresser's Chair

Crystal arrived at the salon at 9:00 am and announced she had walked there! What? It was the first time in years! She would also be walking home in her wedding hair and floor length veil. She had waited her whole life for this day and she was determined to enjoy every minute.

She took her time walking down the street and felt like a princess! It was her big day and everybody on the street could see her in her stunning tiara and wedding veil.

We were invited to her beautiful wedding and I was there to fix her hair, if needed. She thoroughly enjoyed herself and stayed until the very end. The honeymoon was a few months away on purpose, so she could focus fully on her wedding.

Crystal's dream had finally come true. I had never seen her happier! That was ten years ago now and to this day she still drives to my salon to get her hair done. The one and only day she had ever walked there was on the best day of her life!

Life Lesson from the Chair: If you believe strongly enough in your dream, eventually it will come true.

Until next haircut...

Karen Walks Through Fire

Tony Robbins, the famous life coach, peak performance strategist and author, has helped change millions of lives. Including mine!

In 1990, I read both his books and completed his 30-day program, *Personal Power*. I'd often share his insights with my clients, because his ideas and strategies had made such a powerful difference in my life.

Thanks to his "mentorship", I had grown my business from a solo shop to a full service salon with a staff of nine. And I'd achieved a personal goal of losing 60 pounds.

Tony was coming to Toronto to deliver a four-day conference/workshop called, *"Fear into Power"*. It included his famous "Firewalk" experience!

I wanted to go so badly, but there was no way my husband and I could both afford to go. We had young children in grade school. But, I was determined to find a way.

Somehow, I managed to juggle schedules and come up with enough cash to buy my ticket. I wondered how Tony would select participants for his Firewalk and hoped I'd make the cut.

There were over 1000 people at Tony's conference. To my surprise, I found out we were

From the Hairdresser's Chair

ALL going to do the Firewalk!

I froze at the thought of walking barefoot over hot coals. Soon a waiver was passed out, explaining the procedure and the possibility of burns. If we were going to do it, we all had to sign.

Scared to death, I signed it.

Tony was excellent at preparing us. It was the most mind-blowing, exhilarating experience I had ever gone through in my entire life. We practiced all evening in the conference room. He taught us how to put ourselves in the most peak state possible.

We even practiced celebrating prior to the Firewalk. We all went out to see the piles of wood before starting the fire.

My partner was a girl around my age whose company had sent her to this workshop. We were both very nervous, but were determined to go through with it.

We all lined up in rows while we slowly walked over the burning coals. Yes, I said slowly. If we had walked fast, we would have sunk deeper into the coals. Ouch!

At the end of the Firewalk, Tony's staff rinsed our feet with cold water. All I felt was the cold. Then we celebrated like never before!

Later, when I checked out my feet back in my room, they were fine, just a little sensitive. I could hardly sleep, I felt so empowered. My clients are never going to believe I walked barefoot over hot coals!

Tony's Firewalk set us up for the next three days of success training. It was the most incredible weekend I had ever spent in my life. I wish my husband could have joined me. All the way home, tears of joy streamed down my face.

Life Lesson from the Chair: Henry Ford was bang-on when he observed, "If you think you can, you can. If you think you can't, you can't. Either way, you're right."

Until next haircut…

Gracen: A Little Girl Gives All She Can

It was almost twenty years ago that my client, Sara, first had to deal with cancer in her family. It wouldn't be the last.

At the time, she was expecting her first child when her grandfather became ill with cancer. He passed away before his first great grandchild was born.

Sara was so sad that he never got to see her beautiful baby girl, Alexandra. When the baby was only a few months old, Sara learned that her mother was also diagnosed with the disease.

Still devastated by her first loss, Sara then found out her grandmother had cancer. "How can I cope with possibly losing three members of my family on top of caring for a new baby?" she wondered.

It wasn't long before cancer claimed her grandmother, too. Sara and her little one moved into her mother's home.

Despite her fear of losing everyone she cared about, Sara did what she could to stay balanced and hopeful. Every day was a blessing for her Mom to spend time with her new granddaughter, Alexandra.

Sara saw this as a great time of healing for her, although her Mom's nine months of treatment were a challenge and a bit of a blur. Having the baby was their saving grace; keeping them both focused on what was good in life.

Sara's family continued to grow with the welcome addition of another daughter, Gracen, and a little boy, Eric. After ten years had passed, Sara's mother had her final check-up and was declared cancer-free. What a relief!

And do you know that, throughout that whole time, Sara's mother had never told a soul she even had cancer? That's how private she was. I had no idea. I'd done her hair for many, many years and never knew. To this day, she never told her grandchildren.

One day, Sara called me to make an appointment for her daughter. Gracen wanted me to cut all her hair off so she could donate it for wigs for cancer patients. She was only nine years old!

I obliged by cutting off 14 inches of her hair and we packaged up a beautiful, thick ponytail.

Gracen was so excited that she could give her locks to someone who needed a wig. She didn't even know that her own grandmother was a cancer survivor who had worn a wig thanks to the kindness and courage of someone just like her!

That was two years ago. Now Gracen has grown her hair long enough to come in again and donate another 14 inches! Her grandma is so proud of her compassion. She feels blessed that she's here to enjoy all her grandchildren. She knows all of them were her "saving Gracen".

Life Lesson from the Chair: There's no age limit on giving from the heart. We all have something to offer another who might need it more than we do.

Until next haircut…

Marg's Life Goes to the Dogs

Marg was planning to get a puppy. She was considering a golden retriever. Although they're wonderful dogs with a calm temperament, they shed like crazy. You're constantly vacuuming!

I told Marg about a friend of mine, another hairdresser named Fay.

Fay had a beautiful golden named Teaka, who would be in Fay's salon while she worked. Her clients loved Teaka, but after 13 years, the dog passed away.

Marg loved the name Teaka and decided that's what she would name her new dog. Fay was thrilled to know there'd be another Teaka. It helped her feel less sad.

Teaka was the greatest companion! She and Marg enjoyed each other and the years flew by. Soon Marg was talking about retiring from her job at the nursing home. After 30 years, it was getting hard on her physically.

Every hair appointment, the countdown continued until finally she was applying for her pension. She would retire in May, spend the summer with Teaka, then look for part-time work in September. Ideally, she'd work for the school board as a lunch monitor so she'd have time off over the summer and during school breaks.

From the Hairdresser's Chair

"Every day, I tell Teaka that next month it'll just be you and me spending all day together," she told me. Teaka would look up and wag her tail at hearing the excitement in Marg's voice.

By her next appointment, she expected to be a retiree! But, when she arrived in my salon, I knew something had gone wrong. She looked so sad.

"I had to put Teaka down last week," she explained tearfully. "She wasn't herself – off her food, very lethargic. My husband took her to the vet and, when I got home from work, the vet said that Teaka was full of cancer and suffering with no chance of getting better."

Marg and her husband decided it was best to have the vet end Teaka's pain. They said goodbye that night and she was gone.

The next day was Marg's retirement lunch and last day of work. She suffered through it, rather than enjoy it as planned and came home to grieve the loss of her precious Teaka.

Many tears were shed during that hair appointment. We started chatting about another dog. I got out my laptop and we looked at rescues because Marg didn't want another puppy. Seeing all the Goldens in need of a home seemed to make Marg feel better.

A couple weeks later, Marg emailed to say she had decided on a puppy after all. She figured retirement would give her the time needed to properly train a puppy. She named her Pailie.

This dog is no Teaka. She has a completely different personality, but she brings her own type of joy and she's helping Marg recover from her loss.

Marg and Pailie go for a walk every morning before Marg goes to her part-time job at the school. That worked out as planned. Then she's home again to play with Pailie. They're both enjoying Marg's retirement.

There will never be another Teaka, but there's always plenty of love for the next dog.

Life Lesson from the Chair: *It hurts so much to lose a pet but the joy, love and memory of having one makes that pain worth bearing.*

Until next haircut...

Cindy and Ron Adopt Two Children – and a New Lifestyle

They'd both been single for almost 40 years when Cindy met her ideal man and married Ron. Ten years into the marriage, both seemed very happy. The only thing missing was that they wanted children, but couldn't seem to make it happen.

One day, Cindy confided to me that they were considering adoption. Some people would have questioned why. They had a great life going – travelling when they pleased, no "kid problems" like teachers, homework, sports, sickness, babysitters...not to mention having to look forward to those rebellious teenagers you can't wait to pack off to university!

I was excited for them, though. I knew Cindy had always wanted to be a mom. I could see this wonderful excitement and yearning in her. I told her there are so many joyous experiences with having a family.

- Proud parents, when your child brings home the report card

- Tender, loving moments tucking them into bed at night and they're so open to sharing their feelings and thoughts with you

- Special moments you'll cherish forever: first day of school, the day they graduate, get married or reach a significant milestone

- Just being there for them when they're hurt and need your love and support

The big day finally arrived. Cindy and Ron had been working with FACS (Family and Children Services) for about six months when they were notified about a brother and sister, aged 8 and 12, who'd been in foster care for quite some time and were in need of a home.

FACS thought Cindy and Ron would be a perfect match. Since they were in their fifties, older children would be more suitable.

Cindy was in to get her hair done and said, "We're meeting them tomorrow!" She was excited but very nervous. She asked, "What if they don't like me?"

I replied, "Just relax and be yourself, Cindy. They'll love you!"

That first meeting went well. Before they knew it, the children were moving in.

I told Cindy, "You and Ron have waited many years for this day to come. And these two siblings have waited their whole lifetimes for a permanent home. The timing for all of you was perfect. You were ready, the children were anticipating a Mom and Dad to give them a forever home and the Family and Children Services brought you all together."

I met the children a few weeks later. Cindy brought them in because they needed a haircut! I told her they were all a perfect match and I could see this family blending together with ease.

Life Lesson from the Chair: *While children make the bankroll smaller and the nights longer, they also make love stronger, the home happier and the future worth living for.*

Until next haircut…

126

PART THREE

Angus and Babs: A Love Story for a Lifetime

Bev's parents have been married for 71 years. Angus, 94, and Babs, 92, first met when she was 15 years old. They became friends.

When Babs was working as a clerk in a pharmacy in England, Angus went off to fight in World War II. They wrote to each other for years, continuing to 'date' through their love letters.

Toward the end of the war, Angus was wounded when his battleship was hit at Dunkirk. He lost his spleen. Shrapnel punctured his lung and various parts of his upper body. For nine months, he lay in critical condition in a naval hospital in Dover.

He and Babs kept writing to each other. She even managed a trip to Dover to see him, which was very difficult to do. No longer fit for duty, it was a difficult time for Angus. He had lost his mother and a brother during the war.

By now, he and Babs were completely in love. They married on June 5, 1943 and had three children, including my client Bev.

Angus worked as a toolmaker for many years. During the 1950s, he taught himself electronics and built up a small television repair business, on the side. As a result, he was able to join IBM as a

From the Hairdresser's Chair

Mechanical and Electrical Quality Assurance Inspector, which he did for many years.

Angus and Babs were very adventurous and travelled extensively at a time when few people did. As a family, they toured most of Europe and North Africa during the 1950s and '60s.

When Angus retired, they bought a catamaran, christened the "Golden Goose". He loved the sea and sailed for the next five years. Sometimes, their son would provide an extra set of deck hands.

They sailed the coast of France, around the Channel Islands and put in at ports along the south coast of England. Once, while cruising the French coast, they weathered a really bad hurricane. They made it to safety, but thought they'd lost their boat. However, it had sustained little damage and they were able to carry on.

He and Babs wintered in Spain, in a little apartment in the mountains where they made many friends.

When their daughter, Bev, got married, she and her new husband moved to St Catharines, Ontario. Shortly afterward, her brother left England and arrived in Canada with his family.

By then, Angus and Babs were in their late sixties. They, too, moved to St Catharines, but they weren't finished travelling! They bought a trailer, and travelled around the United States and Canada. For the next ten years or so, they wintered in Florida.

They enjoyed their retirement in Ontario, surrounded by their children, grandchildren and great-grandchildren. Their health was always good until Babs' recent diagnosis of Alzheimer's.

One of the most common forms of dementia, Alzheimer's is a progressive, degenerative disease of the brain that gravely impairs thinking and memory.

Babs had to be placed in a long-term care home. This was devastating to the inseparable couple who were still so much in love. Babs still idolized Angus.

For the first two and a half years, he visited almost every day, bringing her little gifts. Most days, he would have supper with her at the home.

In early 2014, Bev noticed that her Dad had not been looking well. The family got Angus to see a doctor and have some tests done. By fall of that year, they had persuaded him to move in with Babs at the home. He was reluctant to go. He didn't want to give up his independence. Angus was still driving and enjoying his apartment. But he went.

Ten days after he moved into the home with Babs, he was diagnosed with prostate cancer. It had moved into his bones. Just before Thanksgiving, he was told the end was near. Even though Bev was upset, she was relieved that he'd already been moved into the same room as his wife.

Angus was well aware of his situation and wanted to know what was going to happen to him as his time drew closer. They explained they'd keep him comfortable, and as the pain inevitably increased, the nurses would increase the morphine until he would be unconscious. He bravely said, "Do not resuscitate me. Let me go."

As Bev was clearing out the apartment that he and Babs had shared, she found their long-ago love letters. She asked if I remembered those old coil racks that used to hold 45rpm records. Well, she had found one with musty letters from 1938 sitting side by side, in order!

"The tears rolled down my cheeks and I wondered what I should do with them." she told me. "They were not for anyone else to see."

She decided to take them to her Mom after her Dad had passed and offer to read them to her.

I asked Bev, "What do you think kept your Mom and Dad together for over 71 years?" Without hesitating, she simply said, "Love."

Ah...love. Angus and Babs fell deeply in love through their letters and the feeling just grew stronger every day. It got them through some tough times, even war times that, thankfully, many of us will never experience.

Angus died peacefully on Christmas Eve. He may no longer live in Babs' failing memory, but he'll always live in her heart. And in her love letters.

Life Lesson from the Chair: *The truest love endures all things.*

Until next haircut...

Amy Proves that Gratitude is Contagious

Amy is such a joy to have as my client. We have awesome conversations about gratitude and what's good in life. She is always so positive! So one day when she mentioned she had trouble being around her mother-in-law, I was surprised.

Amy said her husband's mother is so ungrateful, it's hard to be around her. She had tried everything she could think of to make her feel more positive but nothing worked.

"If I ask her what she's grateful for," Amy told me, "she says she has nothing to be grateful for and then goes on to complain about everything!"

"Ewe." I thought, "She's a tough one." Obviously, this woman feels unappreciated or maybe even unloved. Amy said she always complains that no one does anything for her, yet that's ridiculous.

"My husband sees her at least twice a week and calls her four or five times during the week. He cuts her grass, takes her shopping, visits with her and she still complains about him!"

One day, I suggested that Amy should try reworking the gratitude question into a gratitude statement. "What do you mean?" she asked.

"Include her in your own gratitude," I explained. "Say something like: I am so grateful to you for _____, and fill in the blank."

Amy agreed to give it a try.

The next month, Amy came in for her hair appointment all excited. "I couldn't wait to come and tell you!" she started. "I had the perfect opportunity to change my mother-in-law's negative energy into a positive feeling.

"Two weeks ago, my husband and I went to visit her. He cut her grass, I helped her do laundry and then the three of us sat down and had a cup of tea together.

"She started complaining about my husband again – right in front of him! I interrupted her and said, 'You know what? I am SO grateful for your son. He's an amazing father to your grandchildren and the most considerate husband anyone could ask for. But what I'm really grateful for is YOU – for raising such a wonderful, caring man. Thank you!"

Amy said her mother-in-law's face turned to stone for a moment. She could barely speak and finally, very softly, she said, "Oh, yes. He is a wonderful man."

Amy said you could tell she felt loved and appreciated. She continued to include her in her gratitude and appreciation as time went on. Before she knew it, her whole demeanour changed within a week.

I think the woman had sat in negative energy for so long, it was blocking anything good. It took

From the Hairdresser's Chair

Amy's inclusion to move her into a better place. I loved her way of doing it.

I decided to give it a try myself when the opportunity arose. What a result I got! I gave my daughter a call one day and she was in a negative mood.

In university at the time, she had too much homework and she was working a part-time job. Feeling overwhelmed and tired, she had lots of complaints.

I said to her, "Michelle, you could change the way you feel." and she retorted, "What if I don't want to?"

Hmmm…there was my opportunity!

It was a Thursday and that Saturday was the anniversary of my Dad passing away.

I interrupted my daughter's complaining and said, "You know, Saturday will be the anniversary of your Grandpa's death and I am so grateful to have had the best Dad in the world. But what I'm REALLY grateful for is that I had his oldest grandchildren. He got to know you well and you were able to spend so much time with him. He loved you so much and I'm so grateful that you were such a joy to him."

Silence on the phone. Did I change the way she felt? Absolutely! Finally, she said, "I'm glad we were older and got to spend all that time with him. He was the best!"

After we hung up, I thought, "Huh! I think now I'll email my son, who lives out West." I wrote him that Grandpa would have died ten years ago on Saturday and I was so grateful he got to spend so much time with him, as his oldest grandson. Grandpa loved you so much and you were such a joy to him!

Well…I received this huge response of gratitude and appreciation from my son. He told me how Grandpa had taught him to drive a car and had taken him fishing. I hadn't even known what mood my son had been in, but he sure was grateful now, with such fond memories of his grandfather!

Amy – I am SO grateful to have had you sit in my chair, inspire and move me by sharing your story. Thank you, thank you, THANK YOU!

Life Lesson from the Chair: There's always something to be grateful for. Appreciating even the smallest things can often create the biggest results and changes. Try it!

Until next haircut…

Barb and Barb: Their Parallel Lives Intersect

For many years, I have done Barb Smith's hair. When she called to tell me her husband, Bob, had died of a heart attack, I was shocked. He was only in his late forties.

It was very sad to see Barb a widow, but she pulled herself together with great support from family and friend. Her career at the university kept her busy and occupied too.

Some time went by. A new client with the same name – Barb Smith – came for a colour and haircut. When she told me her husband's name was Bob, I told her about my "first" Barb Smith having a hubby named Bob, too. I didn't tell her that he had passed on, though. This Barb chuckled and said, "I know we have very common names."

Barb #2 came back a few months later and told me that *her* Bob had recently died of a heart attack. And *he* was only in his fifties!

This eerie feeling came over me. Two Barbs. Two Bobs. Two heart attacks both ending in two untimely deaths. When Barb #1 came in again, I told her about Bob #2. She was surprised and agreed it was a very odd coincidence indeed.

It was a few months later when I finally told Barb #2 about Bob #1. She, too, was shocked. With the permission of both Barbs, I began to share stories of their lives from one to the other. They began to feel connected and I said I hoped that someday they'd meet.

Chances were slim, however. They each lived more than half an hour away from my salon in opposite directions.

One day, I noticed that both Barbs had booked appointments for the same day; in fact, one right after the other! I told both of them that the time had come for them to meet. They were excited but felt a bit nervous.

At last it was Saturday noon. The two Barbs met, looked at each other with tears in their eyes and embraced in a long hug. It was as if they'd known each other for years! They had a lovely first visit and shared so many wonderful stories. Like old friends with a lot in common.

It was a special day in my salon, bringing these two together. I'm so blessed to have not one, but TWO Barbs sit in my chair!

Life Lesson from the Chair: Do you ever wonder why you're here? What your purpose is? You may never truly know. A smile at a stranger, a chance encounter – these seemingly small and insignificant events have the potential power to change someone's life. Let all our acts be kind. We can never be sure who's being affected by them,

Until next haircut...

Linda and Michael Score a Big One on Adversity

My client, Linda, and her husband, Len, raised daughters. There were always dance recitals, pajama parties and proms while the girls were growing up.

Len adored his daughters, but had always longed for a son. Now the couple has four grandsons and they're loving every minute of it.

Linda tells how she and Len always make a point of attending the hockey tournaments their one grandson, Michael, plays in. After the games, they hang around to see him when he comes out of the change room.

One time, they were chatting with a few other parents when all of a sudden, all hell broke loose in the change room. Boys were screaming. Parents were running. What was going on?

Michael had just taken off his skates when the coach walked in with a "hip hip hooray!" because their team had just won. The kids jumped up excitedly. The boy standing next to Michael hadn't yet removed his skates. He jumped up, and then he and his skate blades landed squarely on Michael's toes, cutting four of them in half.

There was blood everywhere. Michael screaming in pain. The coach quickly ran for ice and a towel to wrap his foot. Michael's father scooped him up and rushed him to the hospital.

It had all happened so fast. Linda and Len were shocked when they realized how serious it was and could barely speak as they made their way to the hospital, tears pouring down their cheeks.

When they arrived, Michael's parents had already met with the doctors who decided he needed to go to Sick Kids' Hospital in Toronto where Michael's mom, Becky, had contacted one of the best orthopedic surgeons. He would operate as soon as possible.

The family left immediately for Toronto, relieved they were doing everything they could, but still devastated and worried. What if the doctor couldn't save Michael's toes?

Fear of what could happen threatened to overtake them but they pulled themselves together by turning to their faith. They started praying. Within moments, they felt calm and at peace, knowing Michael was in good hands.

After four anxious hours of waiting for an operating room and two hours of surgery, a doctor came out with the good news. Michael would be fine.

The surgical team had straightened all of his broken toes and then sewn together all the severed tendons. He had two different casts on, and he was not allowed to move his toes at all for two months so the tendons could heal.

They wanted to keep him in the hospital for a few days on strong pain medication and antibiotics, in case of infection.

Michael's parents and grandparents left the hospital about midnight and headed home. Friends had stepped in to take care of their other children. There were many messages waiting for them on their answering machine.

News travels fast in the hockey world! The boy who had jumped on Michael's toes was so sorry, he couldn't stop crying. His parents were offering to help in any way. They all felt so bad.

Two months went by and it was time for Michael's casts to come off. His doctor was pleased with how Michael's toes were healing. The day after his last cast was removed, Michael was taken for hyperbaric oxygen treatments, which also helped his tendons heal.

Later, they took Michael to a sports physiotherapy clinic for treatment, where they'd never seen anyone with this type of injury before. They gave Michael some exercises to do at home. He did them faithfully throughout his five months of therapy.

Michael surprised everyone. He was such a trooper. He complained very little. He knew he had to heal and it was going to take some time.

His dad took him to most of his games, giving him an opportunity to see them from an entirely different point of view. He could see where mistakes were being made and what needed to improve.

He enjoyed watching the games and took mental note of what he saw. Little did he know how much this would improve his own playing in future!

Linda and Len are so proud of their amazing grandson and his positive outlook on life. A year has gone by and now Michael has fully recovered. In fact, he's playing hockey even better than before the accident!

Linda recently emailed to tell me that Michael Miele had won the MVP (Most Valuable Player) award. The newspaper article reads:

> ### Miele's hat trick leads Burlington peewees to Horseshoe title.
> *Miele scored his first marker on a bit of a wraparound on the power play late in the first period. Miele's second goal came a little more than two minutes later off a rebound. Another four minutes later, with Eagles' Bowie in the penalty box, Miele's patience with the puck finally opened up space for him to beat Howe and put Burlington up 4-1."*

From the Hairdresser's Chair

What a great ending to a horrific story. Way to go Michael!

Life Lesson from the Chair: The greatest good often follows the greatest hardship. Never give up or lose hope.

Until next haircut…

Shirley Gains –and Loses – a Daughter-in-law

Shirley was looking forward to her son marrying Miranda, his beautiful childhood sweetheart. Miranda wasn't very close to her own parents and she could hardly wait to call Shirley "Mom". It just felt so right.

Shirley adored Miranda and treated her like her own daughter. Miranda would practice walking down the aisle, a big smile on her face. "Only two more weeks until our wedding and I can call you 'Mom'!" She beamed when visiting her mother-in-law-to-be.

The wedding was fabulous and they had a wonderful honeymoon. Miranda went back to her work as a nurse and life seemed splendid for a few years. Miranda and her husband wanted to have children and felt that they'd be married forever.

One day, Shirley's son came to visit. "Mom, Dad – I have something to tell you. I'm leaving Miranda." They were shocked!

He told them he wasn't in love with her. "There's no one else. We don't fight. She's a wonderful woman, but I only love her as a sister. I'm sorry to do this. But it isn't fair to her or to me. Miranda deserves someone to be deeply in love with her. I'm just not."

From the Hairdresser's Chair

Miranda was devastated. He was the love of her life. She tried everything to convince him to reconsider, but he just couldn't do it. They separated and eventually divorced.

Shirley felt as if a knife had pierced her heart. What could she do? Maintaining her relationship with Miranda would have been very awkward. She lost her daughter-in-law and it was very sad.

Her son moved on and didn't date for quite some time. After a few years, though, he met someone and they married very quickly.

In the meantime, Shirley thought about Miranda all the time. She missed her immensely. She heard from someone at church that Miranda had met someone and was getting married. She was happy for her and said a silent prayer of blessings.

She longed to see her, but she knew her son and new daughter-in-law wouldn't approve. It just wasn't appropriate to rekindle this relationship with her son's ex.

Years went by. Shirley thought of Miranda often and heard that she had two children. Again, she blessed them all in silence and sent warm wishes their way.

Shirley's other son also married, giving her two daughters-in-law. She enjoys her children, their spouses and now her grandchildren, speaking of them often. Although close, the connections were never like the one she experienced with Miranda.

Not long ago, when Shirley came for her monthly hair appointment, she had a big smile, and said, "I have a wonderful story to tell you. Three weeks ago, I needed to go grocery shopping. My husband was busy and I didn't feel like going by myself. (It's Shirley's least favourite chore!). But I forced myself to go. There I was, in the meat department, slowly pushing my cart and looking at products, when I felt something stop my cart."

"I looked up and was astonished to see Miranda! We looked into each other's eyes and it was almost spiritual. She came right over to me and we embraced in the longest, tightest hug!"

Right away, Shirley told Miranda how much she missed her and how often she thought of her. "I always wondered if I did the right thing, staying away while you and my son were divorcing."

Miranda said she had thought the same thing. "I wanted to see you so much, but I thought it was no longer my place. I think of you all the time and have told my husband all about you."

She asked how Shirley and her husband were doing. They and her sons were all doing well. Shirley said, "I hear you have two children. Tell me about them."

From the Hairdresser's Chair

When Miranda replied that they were great, Shirley said, "No! Tell me all about them. Their personalities. What are they like?"

Miranda smiled and said, "Ah. My 9-year-old is smart and loves sports. The 2-year-old is full of energy and so lovable."

As Miranda excused herself saying she had to get home for suppertime, she invited Shirley to drop by for a cup of tea. "I'd love to see you again. My husband knows all about you."

Shirley hesitated and said, "It was lovely meeting you again. Let's hope our paths will cross again someday." She gave Miranda a huge hug and they parted ways.

"I don't think I can go there for tea," Shirley told me. "I'm not sure how my son would feel about it."

I said, "It's been 18 years. Go for it!"

Even though my first husband and I had been divorced for 29 years, I maintained my relationship with his mother until the day she died. Of course, I did her hair and she never stopped coming to me, but my second husband was fine with our relationship and so was my ex.

For now, though, Shirley feels content with her embrace and the few moments she shared with

Miranda. She knows they both had a wonderful connection and she feels blessed for the encounter.

Life Lesson from the Chair: *Divorce is extra hard because it's possible to lose more than just the one person you loved. Someone once wrote that, if you love something, set it free. If it comes back to you, it's yours. If not, it never was.*

Until next haircut…

Sara and Randy Never Say Never

Sara and her boyfriend, Randy, had been happily living together for 28 years. She had been married once before and was determined "never again"! She didn't need to call any man her husband.

Until, that is, she learned that Randy had terminal cancer.

Randy had served in the army for 20 years. Annual physicals were mandatory. Now retired for ten years, he felt that he no longer needed the check-ups. "I never smoked. I only drink occasionally, eat healthy and keep myself in good shape," he reasoned.

Despite Sara's urging, he felt no need to see the doctor although his new career in sales was somewhat stressful.

In 2009, he finally went to see his doctor because he felt so tired he could barely stand. "He told me he couldn't even feel his legs, they were so heavy," Sara told me. "His GP ran some tests and told him he just needed a holiday."

But, Randy knew something was drastically wrong. He would sometimes get sharp pains while he was walking. Then one day, he noticed blood in his urine. Sara asked her pharmacist to recommend another doctor, who ordered the dreaded colonoscopy.

The couple sat hand in hand as the doctor delivered the bad news: advanced bowel cancer. Randy had three large, aggressive tumours. He had thought he was invincible, having survived 20 years in the army. He was only 53 and bulletproof, wasn't he?

The doctor recommended surgery to remove the tumours, but the operation revealed even more of them. Despite having to perform some very creative surgery, the doctors were confident that Randy would be off the colostomy bag in a few months because of his age and fitness level.

At first, Randy couldn't muster the courage to look at the colostomy bag while in hospital. Eventually, though, the cancer's severity required that he undergo chemo and radiation treatments, too. After a very rough year, they finally ended.

After three months, his check-up confirmed that the treatments had failed. Randy decided he'd had enough. "I'm not going to chase cancer!" he declared.

Randy wanted to live the rest of his life to the fullest. To have fun while he could and enjoy life's simple pleasures with family and friends.

He wanted Sara to marry him, so she'd be taken care of financially when he was gone. Even though they'd been together for almost 30 years, she could not be the beneficiary of his pension unless they were legally married for at least one full year.

It was Christmastime. Randy and Sara exchanged wedding vows at 7:00 o'clock New Year's Eve, surrounded by their closest friends and family.

Sara couldn't persuade Randy to have more surgery to remove the latest tumours, and she knew in her heart they didn't have much time left together. She took a leave of absence from her work as a nurse and they had a wonderful year together.

Sara discovered that she loved being a wife to Randy. She made sure he was comfortable and was able to keep him at home until he passed away the following February.

As he wished, Randy was able to continue providing for her through his pension. His greatest legacy, though, will always be that Sara had agreed to marry and had discovered how proud she was to call him "her husband".

Life Lesson from the Chair: Keep your heart and mind open to all possibilities. Never say never again.

Until next haircut...

Louise Becomes a "Holy Hooker"

Meet Louise. She has sat in my chair for 40 years and we've shared many wonderful stories during that time.

Now that she has retired, she has joined her church's "Monday Night Knitting Club". Except the group now calls itself the "Holy Hookers" – a nickname the good bishop found totally hilarious.

You might think a knitting club sounds pretty boring, but Louise and the ladies have a blast. What I love most about her story (apart from the club's nickname) is the reason why they get together to knit and crochet.

The club started with only four or five women. Over the years, it grew to include 35 people. Some came from other churches. Anyone who had leftover wool would donate it to the Holy Hookers. They'd make squares of many brilliant colours and then sew them to make a blanket.

Then they would also make a bag, like a backpack, to hold the finished blanket. A label on the bag would tell the recipient, "This blanket was made especially for you!"

The Holy Hookers would give these blankets-in-a-bag to teenagers who were called "couch surfers", because they had no home and were always in search of a couch or bed to sleep on.

From the Hairdresser's Chair

As the knitting club grew, they also made prayer shawls and lap blankets for nursing home residents; baby blankets for preemies at the hospital; as well as hats and mittens for COPE (Community Outreach Prevention & Education Program).

Doing this gave the women such joy. Louise told me part of the fun was that, "We solve the troubles of the world at our meetings. We learn so much from each other. We're a team and we contribute to our community. It doesn't get any better than that!"

Louise told me about a time when she met one of the couch surfers, while delivering a blanket. He shared his story with her.

His mother was a drug addict who couldn't provide for him so, at age 8, he went into foster care. No one wanted to adopt him, preferring to wait for a younger child. He changed schools seven times in eight years.

But, he had one foster mom who always encouraged him to finish school. She told him he'd been born with a God given gift and he needed to seek out what his purpose in life was.

He always remembered what she had said and he planned to do that. She was his favourite, because she believed in him.

When Louise met him, he'd been living with a nice family for two months. He'd lived with so many different people that year, he said it would be nice someday to have his very own place.

He told Louise he'd be graduating in June. Louise handed him the bag. As he looked at the tag, a tear ran down his cheek when he read, "This was made especially for you". "Wow!" he exclaimed. "I've moved around so much, I don't have very many things. Thank you so much."

Louise knew at that moment why she is a Holy Hooker – it's for moments like that when she sees the gratitude of someone who has had it so rough and who appreciates something so small.

Life Lesson from the Chair: *We all have something to give, even if it's just a smile or word of encouragement. You never know what effect your kindness might have on someone else's life.*

Until next haircut...

Peter's Happy Ending Started Here

Betty looked like she needed a glass of wine. She'd just been through a whirlwind of stress with her family and had been granted temporary custody of her two young grandsons, aged four and 18 months.

Children and Family Services had taken the boys away from her daughter, whose boyfriend was a drug dealer. Betty had five daughters, all out on their own at university and college, except for this one.

Betty and her husband of only seven years had just met with a real estate agent to put their house up for sale and buy a condo. They were preparing for their retirement; looking after two young kids hadn't been part of their plans.

When the two boys arrived, the "for sale" sign came down and a new life began as they found themselves in the role of parents again.

Betty had no idea how long this arrangement would last, but she knew her daughter would never be able to care for these children again and she was concerned for her grandsons' future.

The younger boy, Peter, was proving to be a handful. Betty had a hard decision to make.

She knew that my stepdaughter and her partner (let's call them Barb and Dori) had already adopted a little boy now aged four and were hoping to adopt another.

When Betty came for her monthly hair colour, she announced, "I've made a big decision. I'm going to give Peter up and keep the older brother to raise. I was hoping that Barb might be interested in meeting him and taking him in as a foster child, with a future adoption possible."

Although I was shocked at first, I totally understood. Betty had already raised five children of her own and she was tired. She wanted foster parents she knew for Peter so that she could retain visiting rights. She felt the older boy would be a little easier for her and her husband to raise.

They already had a very strong relationship with him, but she didn't have the heart to hand Peter over to Children and Family Services.

She had seen no improvement in her daughter and Betty knew in her heart that she would never be able to take her children back. She had to think of the boys' future and what was best for the two of them.

I called Barb and planted the seed of Betty's idea. By the next day, she and Dori had discussed it and said they'd like to meet Peter. I arranged it with Betty for the following day.

Barb, Dori and I went over to Betty's where we sat outside on the patio and sipped hot tea as we watched Peter play in the backyard for about an hour. It was mid-March. We usually have snow on the ground at that time of year, but this day was sunny and brisk. Peter's cheeks were rosy; he was full of energy and totally adorable.

Betty and her husband thoroughly enjoyed meeting Barb and Dori. They thought they'd make terrific foster parents for Peter.

Barb and Dori talked things over late into that night. Next day, Barb called Betty to ask for another meeting.

This time, Betty brought Peter to their home to see how he would fit in. For the next two weeks, they met with Peter every other day.

Betty called Children and Family Services to explain the circumstances. Barb and Dori were pre-approved because of their earlier adoption so the transition was smooth and quick. They were now proud foster parents to Peter!

To legally adopt him, though, would require a lot of red tape.

Two years later, Peter got his "forever" home and two parents who adore him. The adoption will be finalized in the very near future. Everyone is so excited!

Betty recently came in to see me for her regular monthly appointment. "I guess you and I are officially grandmothers to the same child now!" she exclaimed. I told her how relieved I was that everything had worked out and the adoption would finally happen. I also told her that Barb and Dori felt so blessed.

Betty loves the pair of them and knows her grandson will have a wonderful life now. Giving Peter up had been a difficult decision for her, but it was best for Peter. Betty has built a warm and loving relationship with his new parents, too.

We smiled at each other with tears in our eyes, knowing that little Peter's journey all started in my hairdresser's chair!

Life Lesson from the Chair: Learn to understand and appreciate that the best things in life often happen when the worst things happen first.

Until next haircut…

Marnie, the Flea Market and Me

Marnie is a travel agent. One day, she asked, "Karen - would you like to share a booth to promote your speaking business with me at the local flea market?"

At first I hesitated, thinking that the flea market is not exactly the type of place for a facilitator to find prospects. But I said yes, because Marnie had volunteered at many of my seminars and had also helped me develop a CD on the subject of attracting more abundance into your life.

We arranged to visit the flea market to see what was available. Now Marnie is a very bubbly, outgoing and cheerful person. When she walks into a room, she gets attention! This was no exception. We met Jim and Jen, who could see how passionate Marnie was about her travel business.

When Jen asked what my business was, I told her that I taught workshops on the Law of Attraction. She and Jim looked confused. "What's that? We've never heard of it."

I briefly explained how "like attracts like" and said that it has to do with energy, vibration, how you feel, emotions and what you focus on. Jim asked for an example. I said, "Right now, I can deliberately make us all feel abundant just by the words I say."

"How can you do that?" Jim wanted to know. Marnie and I looked at each other. She giggled, because she knew where I was going with this. "Last night," I started, "My friend bought me a drink. Two days ago, I saved $8 buying a book. Then yesterday, a neighbour shoveled my driveway." I spoke enthusiastically about the good things I'd received.

Then Marnie picked it up. "My Mom bought me lunch the other day. I received a bigger commission cheque than I expected. Then my husband surprised me by hiring a cleaning lady for a day!" She was bursting with excitement.

Jen was ready to jump in. "Well, I had my dinner paid for last week when I was in Toronto and I got a bonus at work yesterday!"

Jim said, "Hey! It's my turn! Last Friday, I got free tickets to the Buffalo Sabre's game and I didn't even pay for parking!"

Then I said, "Stop!" and looked around at everyone. "Do you feel more abundant right now than you did ten minutes ago?"

Jim said, "Wow! I can't believe how you just changed the way we all feel!"

Between Marine's enthusiasm and my abundance exercise, the next thing we knew Jen said, "I really like you guys. I'm going to give you the double space for the price of a single, front and centre. We normally ask you to book two weeks in a row, but I know you only want one week, so we'll let that go without penalty."

Marnie and I just smiled and said, "Thank you!" Walking out of there, we looked at each other and said, "WOW! Are we ever abundant!" Hmmm...I wonder why?!!

Life Lesson from the Chair: *When you truly appreciate what you already have and remain positive, you'll invite more of the same into your life.*

Until next haircut...

Sherry and Mary Learn the Power of Positive Affirmations

Hairstylists hear it all. Sherry was very upset when she arrived for her appointment one August. A single mom, she felt she was losing control of her mischievous 9-year-old daughter's behaviour that summer. Sherry was very frustrated and losing her patience. Would this ever end?

I noticed that Sherry was only giving her attention to the problem, not the solution. Most people do that. They spend 80% of the time on the problem and only 20% on the solution. I've learned to flip that around.

After listening briefly to her problem, I changed gears. I wanted to shift her over to what she wanted to have happen. What was the solution to Mary's behaviour?

I reminded her of when we were kids and our parents or teachers made us write out lines. Usually, they were negative statements: "I won't steal candy". "I won't talk in class". "I'll never hit my sister again". Every statement we make is an affirmation. Negative or positive.

I suggested that Sherry and I create some positive affirmations. When Mary acts up, Sherry could have her write out lines using a positive statement.

From the Hairdresser's Chair

The best way to come up with positive affirmations is to ask questions like: "Why am I a good daughter?" "Why am I a good student?" "Why am I a good friend?"

When we hear a question, our subconscious automatically tries to find an answer. So having Mary answer these questions would result in positive affirmations that she created.

For example: "I'm enjoying time with my Mom." "I'm consistently handing my homework in on time." "I'm a good listener when I'm with my friends" would be positive affirmations based on the above questions.

It would be even more effective to have Mary come up with her own questions, like: "Why is it so easy for me to be to school on time?" "Why am I a good friend?" "Why did I help the teacher?" "Why do I have good marks?" "Why do I love doing my homework?"

As Mary writes these questions out, she starts to plant the seed of an answer into her subconscious mind which interprets it as a command. Soon, she'll start to receive the results or answers she's asking for. I could see the relief in Sherry's face as we came up with this solution.

She later told me that it worked! She came up with more questions for Mary to answer: "Why am I so grateful?" "Why do I appreciate my Mom?" "Why do I respect my teacher?"

Life Lesson from the Chair: *Next time you have a problem, turn it on its head and spend your time focusing on the solution instead. Problem solved!*

Until next haircut...

Julie Acknowledges a Stranger's Anger

We sometimes need to be validated so our feelings are heard. Yet how often do we acknowledge?

Julie had an interesting experience. As she sat in my chair, she told me she had intervened in a situation in a parking lot. I asked her what had happened.

"Well," she began, "I was locking my car door when I heard some scuffling and some noise. I looked up and saw this man who was screaming at a woman. She had just hit his car with a shopping cart."

"The cart was lying on its side on the ground, with five cases of water in it. The woman was a petite Asian woman with dark, shiny hair and she was having trouble standing up. It looked as if she might have hurt her ankle."

"The man had thinning grey hair. He looked about 60 years old. And his car looked about 10 years old! It certainly wasn't new."

"He was outraged and screaming, 'Look what you did to my car!' He was paying no attention to the possibility the woman might have been hurt."

"People were crowding around to help the woman up, and they lifted the water out of the cart to right it. Everyone told him it was an accident and he should calm down. But he wouldn't listen. He flailed his arms in the air, then slammed them down on his car with such anger!"

Julie said that, since the crowd was helping the poor woman get her bearings, she decided to acknowledge the man.

She walked up to him and said, "Sir, you have every right to be upset here. Look at the dent in your car! It doesn't seem fair."

Once his feelings were acknowledged, he started to calm down. Julie went on, "This wasn't the woman's fault. Look at the large hole in the pavement near your car. First of all, such a petite woman shouldn't have been pushing a heavy cart full of cases of water. The store cashiers should have called for someone to help her."

"The buggy got away from her and tipped over when it hit that hole. I suggest that you and she go back into the store and talk to the manager about this."

The man calmly agreed that was a good idea. After Julie had finished her own grocery shopping, she came out to the lot and saw the man and woman talking together calmly. They had spoken to the store manager and worked out the details.

This resolution may have never happened had Julie not acknowledged the man's feelings during the incident. Once she validated his anger, he felt entirely different toward the accident. He calmed right down and began to think straight, showing compassion toward the woman and apologizing for his outburst.

Think about your last heated discussion. Were you blaming someone for something that had affected you in a negative way? Imagine how things might have turned out differently if you had said, "I totally understand why you're upset. You have every right to be angry or hurt." Pause briefly and then say, "However..." and point out the facts calmly and without judgment.

Lesson from the chair: *Acknowledging bad feelings can result in good outcomes.*

Until next haircut...

Judy's Tale of Three Beds

Once upon a time, I heard a story similar to the fairy tale, *Goldilocks and the Three Bears*, from a client of mine named Judy.

"Before my husband Pete and I got married, he bought the biggest waterbed you've ever seen. This thing was king size – extra-long with a double pedestal frame that had six huge drawers, a massive bookcase-style headboard…you needed a footstool to climb into it!"

"There were four-inch bumpers all the way around it, and you had to squeeze by it to get to the dresser. It took up the whole room!"

It was a full-motion waterbed and she wondered why he had ever bought it, but he just loved it.

The first week Judy slept in it, she said she felt like she was in a boat, hitting big waves. Every time her husband rolled over, this big tidal wave would push her. She learned to ride the waves after a few weeks, and once she got used to it agreed the bed was pretty comfy– cozy and warm.

"But there was no way you could sit up in bed with a cup of coffee without spilling it!" she exclaimed.

After about six months, Judy started getting backaches. Every night, she'd wake up about 3:00

am and head down to the couch. She told her husband they needed a new bed.

"Well, there was no way he'd change the frame, but he was willing to change the mattress," she told me. "The only one we could find that would fit was an expensive air mattress that came with a compressor and a switch to pump it up firm or let air out to soften it."

Ahhh...relief! No more tsunamis or sore backs!

Unfortunately, it only lasted a year before it sprang a leak. Judy would have to pump it up in the middle of the night or it'd go soft and offer no support at all. Trouble was, it sounded like a vacuum cleaner! The noise woke up her husband and their kids would yell for her to turn it off!

Judy said, "It got even worse. Sometimes, the compressor wouldn't work. I'd have to get out of bed, walk to the other side dragging the switch with me, and kick the compressor into action."

This went on for months. Once, during a summer heat wave, they had no power and had to borrow a generator to pump up their bed or it would have been flat as a pancake in the morning.

Judy laughed, "I'd had enough of Bed #2! First the tidal wave, then a sunken ship. We decided to get a normal mattress custom made extra-long and deep to fit this giant waterbed frame."

169

Finally, after five years of marriage, "Bed #3 is just right!" But that was some time ago. Years have passed and then her back started bothering her again. She decided to buy a memory foam topper. "We hated it," she told me. "My husband said it felt like we were sleeping on top of Gumby!" They got rid of the topper, flipped Mattress #3 over and no more backaches!

She jokes "My husband probably wonders why he ever married me and brought me aboard his waterbed. The first year was like a tidal wave, our next few years were like a sunken ship, and our next fifteen years were good until I brought Gumby aboard."

Life Lesson from the Chair: To live happily ever after, be prepared to compromise and work out the kinks. Even the literal ones!

Until next haircut…

From the Hairdresser's Chair

Lori's Sad Story of Love and Regret

Lori's father passed away eight years ago. Her loss was especially sad because he hadn't seen his younger brother, Mike, for 30 years. Mike had had a problem with their parents and decided to distance himself from the whole family.

Many attempts were made to find Lori's Uncle Mike but all failed.

When Lori was 19, she wrote a letter to her uncle, hoping to restore the lost connection with his brother, her Dad.

A few weeks ago, Lori came for her appointment and told me this story. She's now 48 years old and she received a phone call from a lawyer in British Columbia, to advise that her Uncle Mike had passed away.

She, her Mom and her Dad's older brother flew from Toronto to attend the funeral in BC. There, they met a waitress who saw Mike every day in the restaurant where she worked. They became close, but she always believed he was a loner with no family. She was very surprised to learn he had a huge family, but chose to have nothing to do with them.

When Lori and her Mom went to Mike's apartment to help sort out his belongings, they were shocked at what they saw. He was like one of those hoarders you see on TV. You couldn't move in his apartment. There were stacks of books and piles of newspapers - junk everywhere.

Mike had been found dead, sitting in his chair. On the table beside it, were all the letters his brother had sent him over the years. All unopened. And there was the letter Lori had sent him when she was 19. Also unopened.

Tears filled their eyes when they thought of how much their husband and father had missed his younger brother. Even worse, were the pain and loneliness Mike must have felt; knowing there was a family out there for him, yet too afraid ever to reach out.

It broke the waitress' heart to learn all this. Since she was the only one Mike had let into his life, the family decided to give her his car. She was so pleased.

It took a week to clear out his messy apartment. They had a very small funeral, then headed home in sadness for what could have been for Mike.

Together again in Ontario, the family shared how they felt. They needed closure on Mike's death. They all agreed that when you pass, you're surrounded with love. In their hearts, they knew Lori's Dad would be waiting with open arms to welcome his brother Mike. That gave them the closure they all needed in a most bittersweet way.

From the Hairdresser's Chair

Life Lesson from the Chair: There's nothing we can do that the unconditional love of another can't ultimately forgive us for.

Until next haircut…

Laura's Timing is Accidentally Off

Laura drives over an hour and a half to get to my salon. When traffic is good, she can sometimes arrive early.

For one appointment in particular, she was a half hour ahead of time, so she stopped at the corner diner for a coffee. Coming out, she saw someone about to hit her car in the parking lot! She yelled to get the woman's attention, but it was too late.

Emerging from her car, the woman said, "Oh. It's only a scratch." Laura took her name, phone number and insurance details just in case. She didn't call the police, though, because they normally won't come for parking lot fender benders.

The woman who hit her left, and Laura hobbled her car to my salon. The wheel was scraping, but she only had to drive it for a block. However, she was concerned about getting home. She had three children waiting for her.

I started her hair while she called the phone number the woman had given her. It was a taxicab company. Laura explained the situation and found out, to her dismay, that someone had borrowed the cab and wasn't insured!

As I did her highlights, Laura became increasingly panicked. What a mess! No insurance. Yikes! What was she going to do?

From the Hairdresser's Chair

Her husband would be home from work soon, but that was still 90 minutes away from where we were. I felt bad for her so I called my husband to check out her vehicle.

Dave is in the car business, so I knew he would be able to get an idea of the damage. Laura's car had been hit much harder than she thought. There was a lot of damage to the wheel and the vehicle was not drivable. We called to rent a car. Nothing was available in the area.

Laura called her sister who lives 30 minutes away to see if she could drive her home. But her sister's car was in need of a repair, too, so that wouldn't work.

I suggested that we call the police and explain the situation. There was a significant amount of damage and someone needed to pay for it. By now, Laura's hair was the last thing on her mind!

As we finished and went outside to meet the police, it started to snow. It was coming down fast and accumulating. The police took all the information and filed a report.

Poor Laura. Her day was going from bad to worse! I told her she could leave her vehicle and Dave would take it to his mechanic to get it fixed. But there was still no way for her to get home and the weather was getting bad.

Laura's husband decided they should have it towed home and she could ride in the tow truck. Finally, a decision was made! Six hours later, Laura was home with her kids.

What an expensive hair appointment it turned out to be for her! So many unforeseen circumstances. If only she hadn't been early for her appointment!

Life Lesson from the Chair: Our fate and fortune can be changed in a single heartbeat. How we react to the unexpected depends on – and also determines – our character.

Until next haircut...

From the Hairdresser's Chair

Doreen's Many Loves and Losses

Doreen's husband, Pete, had been battling cancer for some time. She would fill me in on his treatments, improvements and challenges. She decided to get two kittens to keep him occupied while recovering at home. Pete loved his little kittens, Tigger and Kalie.

They helped him cope with what was coming. They gave him comfort and kept him entertained. The two would curl up on his lap and drift off to sleep while he rested. But, soon after they grew up, Pete passed away.

Doreen and Pete had a large home on a few acres in the country, where a big barn had housed his workshop and a garage. The property was too much for this recently widowed senior to take care of, so Doreen put it up for sale.

Her three sons helped her get it ready and the two cats were a great comfort to her during this sad time.

The house was sold at Christmas and Doreen would be moving in March. Wrapping gifts in one of the bedrooms, she left a spool of ribbon on the bed. A few hours later, she noticed Tigger had a red ribbon hanging from his mouth! She gasped, "Tigger! What did you do?"

She pulled at the thin ribbon. It just kept coming and coming! Finally, it ended. She couldn't believe how much ribbon Tigger had swallowed!

She decided she'd better have him checked over, so Doreen took Tigger to the vet where an x-ray showed his tummy was STILL full of ribbon! It would cost her $1500 to have it surgically removed. Doreen hesitated, but the only other option was to have poor Tigger put down.

Her grandson, Kenny, burst into tears and begged her to save Tigger. One look at him and how could she possibly say no to the surgery? And so the ribbon-eating cat underwent his expensive operation.

Doreen felt it was her fault Tigger had eaten the ribbon. After all, she'd left the bedroom door open with the ribbon lying out. When she picked him up the next day with fresh stitches in his tummy, she was happy to write out the cheque and bring Tigger home.

March came and Doreen moved into her new condo in a seniors' building. It was perfect for her and she loved it. But Tigger and Kalie took their time adjusting.

(I've heard that a cat would rather stay in the same place and have a new owner, than move away with the current owner. A cat lover may not agree with that. Dogs, on the other hand, are more loyal. They'll go anywhere their owner takes them).

Soon after Doreen had settled in her new home, her son John became ill with cancer. She thought sadly, "Here we go again."

John had surgery and came to stay with Doreen while he was recovering. Losing Pete had been tough enough, but he had lived a full life into his 70s. John was only 42. This didn't seem fair.

One day, John answered the door when Doreen was out. He accidentally left the door open for a moment too long, and Tigger got out. John was too weak to search for him. He felt horrible and wondered if Tigger would come home.

Although Doreen was devastated at the news, she tried not to show her ill son how upset she was. Tigger had been her husband Pete's favourite. She had such fond memories of Tigger sleeping in his lap, putting a smile on Pete's face.

She contacted the Humane Society. No Tigger. Time went by and their favourite feline never came home. They had put posters up in the complex and many people were keeping their eyes out for him.

As Doreen sat in my chair, I asked her, "Was that the cat that swallowed the ribbon?"

"Yes," she replied, "the one I spent $1500.00 on!"

179

Doreen's son, John, was going through many treatments, but the harsh reality was, he was full of cancer. As she sat in my chair, she was so sad. "We're not supposed to bury our children." My heart went out to her as I handed her a tissue.

At her next appointment, Doreen told me, "We lost him." Her daughter and two other sons helped her plan John's funeral. Now she's alone at home, with only her other cat, Kalie, to keep her company.

Grieving for her husband and then her son so soon afterward was very trying on this senior. But Doreen pulled herself together and focused on her family. She went out West to visit her sister for three weeks and that helped her heal.

While she was away, her family checked in on Kalie; keeping her fed, watered and her litter changed. Doreen was happy to see her cat when she got home. Kalie jumped into her lap and drifted off to sleep, as usual. Cats can be such a comfort when people are grieving.

A few years went by. One day, Doreen was looking out the window onto her back deck. She reflected on her life, thinking about the births of her children and grandchildren. The deaths of her husband and son. And about losing Tigger.

Suddenly, she felt a sense of relief flowing through her body and gratitude for all of life's experiences. She felt blessed. She said to me, "I felt like I had been gazing out the window for hours. And all of a sudden there was a cat sitting on the fence."

She jumped up and gasped, "Oh my goodness! It looks like Tigger!" It had been three years since she had last seen him. He looked good and healthy! She carefully moved closer to get a better look and he took off.

A warm, fuzzy feeling came over her and she just knew it had to be Tigger! Later that day, she thought that someone in the area must have taken him in and was caring well for him.

A few days went by and he showed up again. This time, she called, "Tigger! Come here!" She just had to know for sure it was her beloved cat so she moved in closer and started to pet him. She worked her hands down to his tummy and found the scar from his expensive stitches!

Then she found the spot on his ear where he had a special marking. Sure enough, it was her long-lost Tigger.

Tears rolled down her cheek as Tigger rubbed his body against her arm. She knew she had to say good-bye. He had found another good home and he looked so well taken care of. She kissed the top of his head and off he went.

She stood quietly, watching him disappear down the path. She felt overwhelmed with joy, just knowing Tigger was still alive. It was a special day of gratitude for Doreen. Now she felt at peace.

Life Lesson from the Chair: *There's no time limit on hope, love or gratitude. What we sincerely appreciate often comes back to provide comfort when we need it most.*

Until next haircut…

Susan Connects with Spirit

Do you know someone who has a connection with the spirit world? For me, that's my client and friend, Susan. She's a medium who has always had that extra support. She knows she can always tap into her connection with her spirit guides and loved ones in spirit to bring her guidance, comfort and peace.

She also works a lot with angels. When Susan's sons were in their teens, she rarely, if ever, had to worry. In the days before cell phones, she would just check in with them by tapping into their energy. If it was calm, she knew all was well.

Any time she felt a ripple in their energy or anxiousness, she knew it was time to have "her guides call their guides"! She'd get them to call her, come home or send protection around them.

Of course, she couldn't stop things from happening to them, nor would she want to. As Susan said, "We're here on the Earth plane to learn lessons, not live in a protective bubble."

Susan loves being able to connect others with their loved ones in spirit, delivering evidence and information only known to them and confirming who she has connected with. She sees the comfort in knowing that the bond of love continues between her clients and their loved ones.

183

Susan lets them know that they can continue to have conversations and ask for assistance. She is urged by their spirits and guides to let people know how they can connect. It might be by writing in a journal, requesting a visit in a dream, or simply sitting in a favourite chair and meditating with the focus to connect.

She says we need to understand that we are never truly alone. Our souls remain connected and that connection is through the bond of love that we share.

I had the opportunity to enjoy a reading with Susan last June. It created a wonderful connection with my Dad. She revealed his character and provided details that astonished me with their accuracy!

All Susan knew about my Dad was that he had passed away 17 years previously. When she started the reading, nothing seemed to make sense. She suggested that I give her a couple of minutes, then asked me what his name was, so she could ask for him specifically.

Before I knew it, she said she was getting boating, fishing and being on the water. That was my Dad, all right! Those were his favourite pastimes. Growing up, my Dad always had a boat and he'd take us out fishing on Lake Erie. She connected to his spirit with such clarity and told me things no one could have possibly known.

From the Hairdresser's Chair

Just before she finished, Susan smiled and said, "I just received a picture in a frame. It's you, on your motorcycle. Your Dad wants you to know he's riding along with you, keeping you safe."

The tears rolled down my cheeks because I would sometimes ask my Dad to be my guardian angel when I rode. Susan said that spirits like it when we ask for their help and guidance.

I thought to myself, "I only do that on occasion. I think I'll start doing more asking!" I thanked Susan for the reading and felt blessed to have experienced that connection with my Dad.

Just before going to Susan for that reading, I'd taken my final motorcycle test. I didn't pass. I booked another test in two weeks' time.

Every day, I went out to practice. It was the highway test coming up and I wasn't yet comfortable driving on the highway.

Remembering what Susan had said about the spirits liking you to ask for guidance, I would invite my Dad to hop on the back with me and I could feel this sense of security. I asked him for awareness, accuracy, protection, and to keep me safe.

It was amazing how much more confident I felt!

Test day finally came. I arrived early and sat under a tree beside my motorcycle, waiting. For the full hour, I took Susan's advice and connected to spirit.

I talked with my Dad, thanking him over and over again for the protection and awareness he gave me. I went into long stretches of gratitude for having this terrific bike, this perfect day to take my test. I offered lots of gratitude for my Dad and the wonderful things he had taught me.

I thanked him for being there for me that day.

When it was my turn to take the test, I felt so confident, peaceful and full of gratitude. I was ready. I thanked the instructor for the opportunity to take the test again.

I have never felt the elation that I did at that moment. My body felt like it was lifting up and floating. I got on my bike after my instruction. The tester spoke into my headset, "Any time you are ready."

I nodded my head and said out loud, "Dad here we go! (*The instructor couldn't hear me*). Keep me safe, accurate, aware and protected. Thank you, thank you, thank you!"

Down a few streets and onto the busy highway I rode. It felt effortless! I was calm, confident, comfortable and at peace. I had this inner knowing that I would pass and it would be perfect.

From the Hairdresser's Chair

Now it was time to play with the transports on the highway. Again, it went so smoothly. I made all my passes perfectly! Off the highway and back again to the test area, I got the green lights I needed and the red lights I wanted. I had a tear going down my cheek. "Thank you, Dad!"

As I parked my bike and pulled off my helmet, the instructor said, "You passed!" And I said, "I *know*!"

He went on to say, "You showed such awareness, caution, and great head checks. You were very observant. I like that! Congratulations!"

Off I went inside to get my paperwork. I sent a quick text to my husband and daughter to say I'd passed.

My whole day had felt effortless. Now I know the comfort, guidance and peace Susan talks about. That hour of connection and gratitude was amazing. Even though I seldom have a full hour, I do what I can and practice this often. What a great way to start every day!

Thank you. THANK you. THANK YOU!

Life Lesson from the Chair: *It takes so little time to say "thank-you", but sincere and heartfelt gratitude will take you farther and faster than you ever thought possible.*

Until next haircut...

Derek Discovers the Sky's His Limit

One day while she was in my chair, Janet asked me if I knew Bob, the mechanic at the airport in Niagara-on-the-Lake.

"Yes, of course!" I replied. "I've met him a few times and my husband, Dave, sees him every Thursday morning. Dave picks up airplane parts for him every Wednesday when he's in Toronto."

"Well, could you please ask Dave to put in a good word for my son, Derek?" Janet asked. She went on to explain that he planned to study at Mohawk College in August to be an Aviation Technician, and he'd like to do a co-op at the airport during his second semester of high school.

"That airport is the only one within reasonable driving range. Plus, there's only one mechanic and I can't imagine that he'd take on more than one or two co-op students."

When Dave asked me if Derek puttered with car engines, changed the oil or tires, I told him no. He said that would have helped but he'd let Bob know that the boy was very interested in learning the trade.

When Derek got his interview – and scored the co-op placement! – Janet gave Dave a Beer Store gift certificate to show her appreciation for his help.

From the Hairdresser's Chair

Derek just loves his co-op term. Before long, Bob had him changing spark plugs, the oil – he even helped change a propeller. Although Derek didn't have his driver's license yet, he was moving planes around in the hangar.

"With the tow motor?" I asked Janet. "No!" she exclaimed. "He sits in the pilot's seat and moves them!"

Dave suggested that Janet should arrange for Derek to take a FAM (familiarization flight). For only $75.00, he'd have an unforgettable experience! Janet booked the appointment and that day they had very good weather.

Arriving at the airport, Janet sat back and watched as Derek and the pilot, Mark, did the walk-around – a full check on the outside of the plane. When Derek said, "Mom, this is the same plane we changed the prop on!" Janet asked if they could take a different plane, please.

Mark laughed and said it would be fine. "No worries. Bob checks over everything his students do."

Walk-around completed, the pilot then sat in the cockpit and went through his full checklist – three pages long on a clipboard. That made Janet feel safe!

Mark told Derek that HE would be taking off. Derek froze in panic at the thought. Coming over to his Mom, he told her and she said, "Hmmm. I think I'll sit this one out!" Mark assured her, "C'mon! He'll be fine. There's dual everything. I'll take over if I need to."

Janet thought, "Whew! Okay. I'll go." She sat in the back and Mark handed her a headset. Derek was sitting in the left seat, Mark in the right. That seemed backward to Janet and she felt very nervous.

Derek had no problem taxiing out to the runway because he had already had experience moving the planes. You steer the plane using your feet on the rudders, not gripping the yoke with your hands as you would a steering wheel. Now they were lined up with the main runway.

The instructor was given the go-ahead over the intercom and said, "OK, Derek. Full throttle, steer with your feet and when the speed reaches 60 knots you are going to pull back gently on the yoke."

Janet's mouth was dry, she was so nervous. Derek took off without a hitch; he was exhilarated. Mark had him climb to 2100 feet and do a large circuit outside the airport. It was like a big square. Then Mark had Derek slow down the throttle; it was time to descend.

"Not too much. You can't go below 80 knots or the aircraft will stall!" Janet's heart skipped a beat in the back seat. Derek lined up the runway and Mark took over, to Mom's great relief.

It was an amazing experience! Derek and Janet both loved it. Now Derek knows he has chosen the right profession. Although he enjoyed the flight, he really likes to work on the planes.

On the drive home, Janet turned to her son and said, "Wow! You took off in a plane and you don't even have your driver's license yet. I'm so proud of you!"

Co-op placements are great for students. Giving them a hands-on experience helps them know they're choosing the right career. Over the years, I've had many co-op students in my salon. I could always tell who would be a great hair stylist and who wouldn't.

When grading them, I always wrote honest comments and recommendations. I'm sure Bob will do the same. For now, he thinks Derek is doing a great job!

Life Lesson from the Chair: Sometimes you have to take a chance on someone who may appear less qualified than you'd like. You can always teach people the skills, but you can't infuse anyone with enthusiasm, energy or a good attitude.

Until next haircut...

PART FOUR

Barbara Hikes the Inca Trail

We all know at least one person who lives life to the fullest. For me, it's my client, Barbara. She's in her mid-seventies now and I've enjoyed doing her hair ever since she moved to Ontario in 2002.

Barbara loves to travel and manages to experience the world in an economical way. She has friends and relatives all over. She uses her Air Miles to visit but never overstays her welcome and always returns their hospitality.

Thirty years ago, she and her first husband were living in Colorado. (She was widowed for a time and then remarried). Their children were young teens when the family took in an exchange student from Peru.

Rae lived with them for 18 months and they all became very close. When Rae returned home, they kept in touch over the years through mail and now email.

Barbara's daughter is now grown and married with kids of her own. She and her family were able to take six months off work to travel. One of their stops was in Peru, where they were to hike the famous Inca Trail. Barbara and her husband were invited to join them.

The Inca Trail is quite strenuous. You have to be fit to complete it. At the time, Barbara was 68 and her husband was 75. She was in good health, walking many miles a day but he didn't feel up to the trek.

Barbara packed her bags, taking walking sticks and a pair of good hiking boots. I did her hair for her just before she left. She gave me a big hug and said, "Just in case I don't make it back."

I knew she was a bit nervous about the hike, but what an experience she'd have! And they'd arranged to see Rae and his family for the first time in 30 years! Rae was ecstatic they were coming. Their plan was to hike the trail and then relax with Rae and his family.

They arrived at the destination to start the trail. It was a 5-day trip, camping in small tents with just a makeshift toilet. Barbara was still a little apprehensive and concerned about the elevation reaching 14,000 feet. Would she have the strength to keep up with the group? She pushed that thought to the back of her mind and looked forward to her adventure!

Here's what she shared with me from her travel diary.

> *The Inca Trail to Machu Picchu. Nov. 12, 2007*
>
> *Day one. Our guides, Fabrizio and Disnarda, explained the whole trip and*

also gave everyone their signature blue backpacks for the trip. That first day, the trek wasn't incredibly difficult or challenging. It was 11 km and mostly flat except for the last hour which was mostly up hill.

After 6 hours, we landed at our camp. It was on a grass ledge that overlooked the trail we'd just accomplished. Then we looked straight up at the next day's climb. It was completely uphill to 'Dead Woman's Pass'.

When we reached our tents to rest, the porters brought us a cup of tea and a basin of hot water to rinse ourselves off before dinner. They served us trout and veggies. It was delicious!

We woke the next morning to our guide giving us cocoa tea and a basin of warm water. We had scrambled eggs with peppers and onions and toast for breakfast. Yum!

That day, we went straight up for 5 hours. What was amazing were the porters carrying 25 kilos of our supplies! We finally reached the top of Dead Woman's Pass. What a relief!

From the Hairdresser's Chair

It was so beautiful. I just sat in awe. The Andes Mountains are truly so gorgeous. We could see green tents set up for us in the valley, so we headed down to them. The porters put our bags in the tent and had supper prepared for us.

When we woke up next morning and unzipped the tents, we found we were sleeping in a bed of fog. It lifted after breakfast and we started our day's walk. About 45 minutes into it, we came across a temple, a sacrificial altar. It was amazing to see all the history of the Trail.

The temple was a kilometer from the top of the next pass and, for the rest of the day, it was downhill. In the valley, we entered a cloud forest full of beautiful exotic plants and flowers.

It was called the cloud forest because this part of the trail literally IS in the clouds. It was damp and colourful with plants of different shapes, sizes and colours growing every which way.

Then we discovered the Inca Tunnel through a huge piece of solid rock – the only way to Machu Pichu.

When we arrived in camp the third day, it was too foggy to see where we were and what we were in for. We were lying in our tents when the fog lifted.

We unzipped the tent and right there in front of us - directly across at eye level - were snow-peaked glaciers coloured pink by the setting sun. It was the most beautiful thing I have ever seen! It seemed so close you could reach out and touch it.

One of the other trekkers said there is a spectacular mountain vista just a 5-minute walk up, so we went up the hill for a 360° view of everything around us. You could see forever and there was the back side of Machu Picchu. What a night to remember!

The next morning was our last day. The fog was heavy, and it was time to say good-bye to our porters. We had small thank-you gifts for them. They sang a song in Spanish to thank us!

After lunch, we saw a beautiful Inca structure that was very well preserved. We found a comfortable spot overlooking the Urubamba River for a nap.

At 4 o'clock, we arrived at the Sun Gate and our first view of Machu Picchu. I was so overwhelmed with amazement and sadness that I started crying because I didn't want it to be over already."

From the Hairdresser's Chair

I love hearing about Barbara's adventures. She inspires me to have more of my own!

Barbara's regret about leaving the Inca Trail was soon replaced with the excitement she and her daughter felt, anticipating their visit with Rae after 30 years.

They arrived at his modest home at noon, to a very warm welcome. Rae's wife and five children were eager to meet the family who had been kind to him so many years ago.

After being treated to lunch, Barbara wandered into the living room. There, on the mantel, were framed pictures of her and her children from 30 years ago! Rae told her he looks at his US experience every day and is so grateful that a family like Barbara's took him in.

Barbara's eyes filled with tears. She never realized how important her family had been to these people.

Three days later, she was off to the airport to head home. Her daughter, son-in-law and grandchildren still had a month left on their world trip. They were going to Hawaii to visit Barbara's son in Maui.

When Barbara came to my salon for a haircut, she shared her fascinating story with me. I asked her, "So what was the highlight of your trip?" Teary-eyed, she said, "Seeing those pictures on Rae's mantel."

Barbara has always been a very giving, caring person. She currently donates her time at a store called Ten Thousand Villages which helps support third world countries. I feel blessed to have her in my chair.

Life Lesson from the Chair: I truly believe in karma, that what goes around comes around. Look how Barbara's hospitality to a stranger like Rae turned out affecting so many lives in a positive way.

Until next haircut...

Amy and Greg Fix Their Broken Relationship

Amy and Greg had been living together for three years and had a strong, solid relationship. I thought they were perfect together. Every appointment, I'd hear how great their relationship was and how they were blending their families with ease.

Every year, they'd travel two or three times to Europe. Their vacations sounded fabulous. Italy and Portugal were their favourite places to visit. Amy was so positive about her life with Greg, she knew they were soul mates.

Then one day, Amy came in for her appointment and told me, "I'm getting tired of Greg complaining about everything! Nothing seems to please him. He shuts me out and never listens to me anymore."

Whoa! It wasn't at all like her to complain about Greg. Next appointment, she announced that they might be breaking up. "We just don't seem to communicate and he's not willing to compromise," she sighed. "I don't know what to do. He's just not flexible."

I knew better. I thought, "The two of them are giving all their attention to what they don't like in their relationship. That just gives you more of what you don't like."

To Amy, I suggested, "Let's do an exercise."

201

I gave her a piece of paper and drew a line down the middle. "Now list ten things you don't like about life with Greg right now in the left column."

After she wrote down ten items, I said, "Okay, good. Now we're going to go through them one by one, and in the right column, you're going to write what you DO want or would like."

She did that, giving herself a list of what she wanted in the relationship; the things that filled her needs. Then I said to her, "We'll cross out what you didn't like now, because we're not going back there!"

Amy said she was already feeling better about Greg. "This is great, but what do I do next?"

I told her to go home and have Greg do the same thing. "When he's finished, you'll each have a list of ten things you want and need in your relationship. After that, you communicate, compromise and only talk about what you DO want."

Off she went, feeling inspired and hopeful with this exercise. I use this type of exercise in workshops to help people achieve clarity so they can move forward. In Amy's case, the goal was fixing a relationship in need of repair.

Next month, she entered my salon with a big smile on her face. "How's Greg?" I asked. She replied, "He's wonderful! We're both great. Thank you! That exercise was amazing. It brought so much clarity to what we both wanted and that has become our focus now."

A few months later, Amy asked me, "Do you think Greg and I are good for each other?"

I chuckled and answered with my own question. "Do you think I would have bothered putting you through that detailed exercise if I didn't think you were a great match? You were meant to be together. You just needed some help in seeing it for yourself."

I see too many people spending 80% of their time on the problem and only 20% on the solution. That just leads to more problems, more disruption and conflict in the relationship. Ultimately, perhaps a break-up. It's too easy today just to end things and look for someone else.

Life Lesson from the Chair: You can't change your outer world until you change your inner world. You'll attract whoever you are; check in with yourself and see what you have to offer. If you want someone sincere, honest, reliable, attentive, generous, ambitious, loving and more, you have to be that way yourself, first. Because like attracts like.

Until next haircut...

Sadie Does a Friend a Big Favour

Sadie has been coming to me for years. We've built a lovely friendship and we both look forward to her monthly appointment.

We check in with each other to see if we lost the few pounds we promised each other we were going to lose that month. It keeps us accountable and this has helped us both stay close to our goal weight!

Over the years, we've shared so much about family, travel, hobbies and many other interests. Sadie travels from the States to have her hair done and I've often mentioned her to my husband, Dave.

One day, car dealer Dave said, "I have a trailer coming in from Florida, and for some reason, the paperwork wasn't completed on time."

"The border needs 72 hours' notice and there was a glitch in the system. It will be arriving on Friday, but I can't pick it up until Monday, according to the customs policy."

"Could you possibly ask your client from the States if I could leave the trailer at her house for the weekend?" He said that there was a motorcycle stowed inside the trailer, but she didn't need to know that because everything was insured.

I thought, "Hmmm. That's a pretty big favour to ask of a client. I'd better ask through email so she has time to think about it." I explained the size of the trailer and told her it was insured. I said that I realized it was a lot to ask and it may or may not work for her, so please be honest.

Soon after, she replied. "It's perfectly fine with me, but I'll need to check with my husband."

The next day, I got an answer. "Yes! Please park the trailer to the left of the garage. Tell your husband he'll see the spot. Here's our address."

I gave Dave her cell phone number and gave Sadie his. This was still a little out of my comfort zone, but everything was set.

The trailer arrived on schedule that Friday afternoon. Dave went over the border, picked it up and delivered it to my client's home. He called her to make sure he was at the right address and all was good.

On Monday, he picked up the trailer as planned and had little trouble getting it across the border to his car lot. I was relieved it was over and all was well.

A few weeks later, Sadie came in to get her hair done. She laughed, "You should have seen the look on my husband's face when I asked him about that favour!"

"In a loud voice he asked how well I knew this hairstylist. 'How can you trust her? Her husband could be a drug dealer for all we know! That trailer could be full of drugs or something illegal. This doesn't sound like a good idea to me!'"

Sadie said she calmed him down and told him that she knew me very well and had met Dave. We'd been friends for years and she felt very comfortable storing the trailer for the weekend.

Then Sadie's husband asked, "How old is this guy?" When Sadie told him Dave was 65, he said, "Oh well, in that case, that's fine." Sadie said to me, "As if age makes a difference whether or not you're a drug dealer!"

We both had a good chuckle over that. When I told Dave about their conversation, he understood the other man's reaction. There really could have been anything inside that trailer!

Even though it all ended well, I decided that would be the last favour I'd ever ask of this client!

Life Lesson from the Chair: *Never agree to do anything that makes you feel uncomfortable just to maintain a friendship. Real friends will share their feelings honestly, without fear of being judged or losing trust.*

Until next haircut...

Deborah Dares to Do Her Bucket List

I love the idea of a bucket list, don't you? That's a list of all the things you want to do before you "kick the bucket". I've had one for years. I look forward to each and every adventure on my list.

I often ask my clients what's on their bucket list. Some aren't sure; they just take one day at a time and let life happen. Not me! I like to visualize all the things I want to do.

My client, Deborah, has a bucket list. One of her big goals is for five years from now. She plans to take a year off and move to Italy where she'll rent a little house or apartment and write a book.

I just know she'll do it, too! She has a long history of achievements. As a single mom, she raised four kids on her own with no financial help or father in the picture for her kids.

She's had her share of financial challenges, but her belief is not to worry about the money. It always shows up somehow, somewhere.

Her other challenges have been getting through her children's adolescent years, which were emotionally draining to her, as a single parent. But, Deborah firmly believes everything happens for a reason and it will all work out. She keeps herself positive through all unforeseen circumstances.

In the next couple of years, all her kids should be through school and on their own. She plans to sell her huge house and property, move into a small condo and spend that year off in Tuscany.

Would you say she's thinking BIG? Absolutely! I know she'll do it, too. Right now, she's working full-time, doing her Master's degree and teaching part-time at a college in the evenings. She's a very driven woman.

Over the years, she's been remodeling her home, getting it ready to sell. Every day, she visualizes her goal. Her decision to live in Tuscany was inspired by the movie, *Under the Tuscan Sun*, which she watches often to affirm her vision.

She shares her dream with everyone in her life. She knows what her place there will look like. She sees the whole picture in detail and she has a big WHY attached to it.

Coping with life's challenges is tough, but Deborah always says, "I keep my eye on the prize."

She's getting through her Master's degree by visualizing that she's already achieved it. Italy is getting closer and she never, ever wonders, "What if I can't pull this off?" She just keeps this knowing in her heart that she will be there.

Deborah inspires me to think BIG. I will be piggybacking on her goal and plan to spend two weeks with her in Italy. One of my other goals is to be a bestselling author.

When you have a big enough WHY and you can see yourself already doing what you're visualizing, the people, things and circumstances start showing up to help move you toward your goal.

Some people think life just gets in the way. You know you've got to take out the garbage, pay the bills, drive the kids to soccer, clean the basement ... Insert your own excuses here!

Life Lesson from the Chair: There will always be chores. Think BIG, know your WHY and keep your eye on the prize!

Until next haircut...

Claude Hurts Then Heals

Why do we so often hear about seniors falling and breaking their bones easily? Lisa is a client of mine who has two daughters, both married with children. The elder, Breanne, has five kids and they live about an hour away from Lisa.

When the children are sick or their parents are away for the weekend, Lisa often goes up to watch them. But, Breanne's in-laws, Dora and Claude, live much closer and are a big help. After all, having five kids today with both parents working full-time isn't easy.

Two of their boys are in hockey, their two daughters take dance and one takes piano lessons and the other is a cheerleader. Although the youngest son is only two, he's sure to be at the arena soon, too!

Now retired, Claude is a huge help. He's always driving the boys to hockey, taking the kids to Sunday school and church every week or appointments after class. Whatever the activity, you can bet Claude is involved.

One winter day, the weather was wild; snow and ice. Claude's wife, Dora, had gone to bed early and he had already shoveled the driveway. Looking out the window, he decided he should put salt on the sidewalk too, so it would be clear in the morning.

He headed outside. As he was applying the salt, his feet went out from under him and he crashed on the ice. He was stunned for a few moments, then got his bearings and started to call for help. There was no one around.

He managed to pull himself up the side of the house, but the pain was excruciating. He couldn't move. He yelled again for his wife. Still no answer.

Claude reached a window and tried kicking it, to make noise. Still no help! He finally made his way back into the house and collapsed, exhausted, on the couch. He took a deep breath and screamed for Dora. Nothing but silence.

Seeing his cell phone on the coffee table, Claude managed to dial 911. The paramedics arrived, put him on a stretcher and Claude said, "You'd better tell my wife that you're taking me to the hospital!"

The paramedics entered her room with a flashlight. "Dora! Wake up! I'm a paramedic and I'm taking your husband to the hospital."

Poor Dora thought she was having a bad dream! When she realized what was happening, she thought Claude had had a heart attack. Once she calmed down, she got dressed and went to the hospital.

Claude was vomiting, the pain was so bad. They immediately sent him in for an MRI and found that he had broken his pelvis. They couldn't believe how he had even walked along the side of the house.

This type of injury cannot be fixed with a cast or surgery, only therapy. Claude was in a wheelchair for a while and the therapy was excruciating. While they encouraged him to do more at home, he found he couldn't. It just hurt too much.

Claude was devastated that he could no longer be involved with his grandkids. He was just too uncomfortable to attend any hockey games.

He knew he needed to be patient in order for his body to heal. Dora had to learn to be extra-patient, too, because Claude's injury was making him so miserable.

Angry, frustrated and hurting, he was taking it out on Dora. Meanwhile, she was doing everything she could to make him more comfortable.

There's a saying, "You always hurt the ones you love." Deep down, we feel the ones we care about most love us unconditionally and will always be there for us. So we can often take them for granted. At the same time, we need to feel appreciated.

Poor Dora was being very patient with her miserable husband. Claude really needed to let her know how thankful he was to have her.

The turning point came when his oldest grandson was to be confirmed. Claude was very pleased that his son and daughter-in-law were keeping their faith and commitment to raising their children in the church, so this was a special event he just had to find a way to attend.

He told no one but Dora of his plans, because he wanted to surprise the rest of the family, especially his first-born grandchild.

212

From the Hairdresser's Chair

Dora managed to dress him in his suit (he couldn't possibly attend church without a suit on!), drugged him up a little bit with pain medication, and wheeled him in just before the ceremony started. She parked him at the back of the church.

Once the children were about to go up to the communion rail, Dora wheeled him up front so he could see everything.

Claude's grandson turned around, a big smile on his face. "Grandpa! You made it!" At that moment, all Claude's anger, disappointment and frustration melted away. The old Claude was back – happy, content and overjoyed to be there with his family!

Patience is a virtue, sometimes defined as "calmly tolerating delay". That certainly describes the saint Dora was! Calm and quiet, but helpful and so patient.

Life Lesson from the Chair: Always try to show kindness in another's trouble and quiet courage in your own.

Until next haircut…

Joyce Gets an Apartment and a New Lease on Life

It was a Saturday morning and I was finishing Joyce's hair when my next client, Becky, arrived early. Joyce and I kept chatting. She was newly separated and would soon be looking for an apartment in Fort Erie.

Overhearing this, Becky said, "My husband rents out apartments in Fort Erie! Would you like his number?"

Joyce said yes, she would, even though it would be some time before she'd need one. Her mother was 95 years old and lived in a seniors' apartment. Because she had just separated, Joyce had stored her belongings at her sister's place and was sharing her Mom's small apartment with her.

It worked out perfectly because Joyce worked shifts in Buffalo. She'd leave for work at 11:30 pm and come back at 8:30 the next morning. That way, the two were able to take turns sleeping in the one bed, and Joyce was there during the day to care for her Mom.

On weekends, Joyce simply slept on the couch.

It was the perfect arrangement for both of them. Joyce could spend quality time with her mother in her later years and her Mom really appreciated Joyce's help because she was getting feeble.

214

Her health insurance wasn't generous enough to cover long-term care in a hospital. Nursing homes were too expensive, too, for someone on such a low income. But her apartment was subsidized and only cost her $110.00 a month.

Soon Joyce decided to call Becky's husband to enquire about his apartment in Fort Erie and put her name on his list for a one-bedroom. They were hard to get. He had many apartments in town, including a small four-plex right on the Niagara River that Joyce would like.

She asked him to contact her if the one-bedroom became available.

Time went by and Joyce's Mom's health was deteriorating. They'd pray together every night, with Joyce always giving thanks that her life circumstances had brought her back home just when her Mom had needed her most and they were able to spend this time with each other.

One day, Joyce received a phone call that a one-bedroom had become available for the first of the month in the smaller building on the Niagara River. It was exactly what Joyce had wanted!

She'd been able to save some money while staying with her Mom. She took it immediately and paid her first and last month's rent.

Then she got her key and started moving her things out of storage. Within a few weeks, her new apartment was ready, but she never slept over there. She wanted to be with her Mom.

Yet again, the timing was meant to be. Her Mom took a turn for the worse, ended up in hospital for two days, then passed away peacefully.

Joyce was ready for her passing, and even though she felt sad, she was so very grateful for the time she'd been able to spend with her mother. After the funeral, Joyce emptied the apartment she and her Mom had shared and donated most of the things to the needy.

At last, she walked into her new apartment, ready to start a new chapter in her own life. She felt completely at peace with her mother's death. She prayed again and gave thanks for the timing of all the events of the past year.

Life Lesson from the Chair: There are times in all our lives when we realize that we were moved like pawns on God's chessboard, to be exactly where He needed us to be for reasons we never saw or understood until later.

Until next haircut…

From the Hairdresser's Chair

Lee's Blind Date – Where Everything's Jake

One day my client, Lee, asked me if I'd ever been on a blind date.

"Yes, once. But it didn't work out," I admitted.

"Well," she said, "I went on a blind date 35 years ago. My girlfriend, Kate, was dating a guy named Larry at the time, and he asked her to set up a blind date for his friend, Jake, who was coming to visit from Sarnia. They were both funeral directors and they'd met at university."

Lee told her friend sure, why not? She was only 17 at the time and it was her first blind date.

They had a blast going to Old Fort Erie and then out for pizza afterward. "Funeral directors are so much fun!" Lee chuckled. But Sarnia was three hours away, so she and Jake never saw each other again.

"You won't believe what just happened, though," Lee continued. "Remember when my husband and I bought that new house and moved in two years ago?"

"Yes," I said. "You told me you love the neighbourhood."

Lee explained that her daughter and their neighbour's son had become best friends. They were inseparable. They even played baseball together and the boy's father, Jake, was their coach.

A couple of weeks ago, Lee noticed that someone had stolen the flowers she'd just planted in her front garden. "I was upset. I saw Jake across the street and went over to vent with him."

He was very sympathetic and told her that someone had stolen all the new shrubs from the front of his friend Larry's funeral home, too. They shook their heads and agreed it was a shame.

"Later that evening, I remembered my blind date with the funeral director 35 years ago!" Lee exclaimed. "I thought it couldn't be the same person so I phoned my friend Kate and asked if she remembered that guy's name. She told me it was Jake Johnson. It WAS the same guy!

"I told her he lived across the street from me and his kids were best friends with mine!"

Kate remarked, "What a coincidence! You both have kids the same age, too. That's pretty unusual if you ask me."

Lee said she wondered about when to tell her husband and her neighbour, Jake. The timing had to be perfect and she couldn't wait to see the look on their faces.

From the Hairdresser's Chair

A week later, she and her husband were at one of their daughter's baseball games. Afterward, her hubby invited Jake to their house for a beer. "This is it," Lee thought.

As the guys were enjoying a beer in the backyard and the kids were swimming in the pool, Lee asked Jake, "Do you remember a blind date about 35 years ago?" She filled him in on the rest of date.

Shocked, Jake answered, "I remember it well. I can't believe it and here we are neighbours!" While the guys got quite a laugh out of it, their kids both said, "Ewww. Our parents went out on a date together. Yuck!"

That was 15 years ago. Today, their two kids are still best friends.

Life Lesson from the Chair: *Always be kind to everyone you meet. You never know when you might meet again!*

Until next haircut...

Elaine and the Pilot Who Wasn't

My husband, Dave, is a pilot and flies a 4-seater 177 Cessna Cardinal out of the Niagara District Airport in Southern Ontario. Usually twice a year, he goes on a getaway with some of his pilot buddies to Cape Hatteras, a small fishing village in North Carolina.

The guys have also been as far as Key West, Florida in a single-engine plane. One time they flew across the ocean to Bahamas. They're pretty adventurous!

One spring, their adventure was to the Florida Keys. A group of three planes and a few new pilots were joining them.

One of them was a guy named Joe. He'd been hanging out at the airport and showed some interest in taking lessons. He wanted to come along. Dave and his buddy, Rick, had room in their plane so they invited Joe to come experience this trip.

Taking extra people made the trip more economical because they'd share expenses. Fuel costs can really add up on a trip this far. You could fly commercially for almost a third less.

While away, Dave would call me near the end of each day. Knowing they were safe, I could sleep better at night!

From the Hairdresser's Chair

I started to notice that, with every phone call, I'd hear many complaints about this new guy, Joe. For some reason, he was annoying everyone.

I'd been sharing Dave's flying adventure with my clients. One evening, Dave phoned while Elaine was in my chair and she encouraged me to take the call. She wasn't in a hurry.

I chatted briefly with Dave. As I finished working on her hair, I told her what he'd just said about all the guys being fed up with this new guy, Joe's, behaviour.

Apparently, when they'd arrived at their hotel, the desk clerk said it would be an hour or so before their rooms would be ready.

The guys said that was fine. They'd go have some lunch. Then Joe went back to the desk clerk and told him they'd need the rooms sooner because one of their group had a severe heart condition and needed to rest.

When he rejoined the guys at lunch, he proudly told them what he had done. They were so annoyed! First off, it wasn't true. And they were hungry, so they wanted some lunch while they waited anyway. And that was just the start of Joe's odd, annoying behaviour.

When my husband came home, he said that was the last time they'd ever bring Joe along. He proved to be an extreme exaggerator and a liar. He told everyone that their plane was his and he'd done them a favour by bringing them along. Can you imagine the nerve?

The guys discovered that he stretched the truth far too often.

A few months went by and Elaine came back for another appointment. She's been married for years and has a beautiful son. I knew she'd been divorced many years ago, but we'd never talked about that before.

This time, though, she was chatting about how she and her ex-husband had owned three fast food restaurants. What a coincidence, I thought. That annoying guy, Joe, who had flown to Florida with Dave and his buddies had the same first name and said that he'd owned three fast food restaurants. I asked Elaine what her married name had been then.

Sure enough, it was the same guy! Elaine's mouth dropped open. "Now you know why I left him!" she exclaimed. "We were only married six short months. We had dated briefly and got married. He lied all the time. It's funny, all those things you mentioned on the trip your husband was on, matched the behaviour of my ex."

I still can't believe it was him. No wonder she'd divorced him.

From the Hairdresser's Chair

Elaine said, "Poor guy. He just doesn't get it. Life, I mean. Being honest will get you more respect even if you are a little annoying in other ways."

I told Elaine that I had many strange coincidences happen in this chair, but this one had to take the cake!

Life Lesson from the Chair: Mom was right – honesty really is the best policy. Liars need good memories. They nearly always trip up and only make themselves look bad. Never lie to anyone, including yourself.

Until next haircut…

.

Jeff's Timing is Perfect

Jeff had just been laid off from his job, broken up with his fiancée, sold his house and had nowhere to live. Then his Mom, Cathy, called from Medicine Hat, to say that his stepdad had just passed away after a lengthy illness. Could he come out to Alberta?

Although sad, the timing was perfect. After staying with his Mom for a few weeks, Jeff decided to pack up his life in Niagara and move west to live with her. He and his 100-pound Rottweiler, Cane, started off on their long road trip.

Jeff adored Cane, but, when they were just a few hours away from their first stop at an aunt's house, he noticed that the Rottie wasn't feeling well. He was panting hard and seemed to have a fever. It was getting late on a Sunday evening. Where could he find an open animal hospital?

He searched for a vet on his GPS and managed to find one, but it would be expensive and Jeff didn't have much money. However, Cane needed his help. The vet worked quickly and discovered that Cane had inhaled some asbestos somewhere. He'd been minutes away from dying.

She had saved his life and Jeff phoned his aunt in tears, to tell her what had happened. Without hesitating, she paid the $1200.00 vet bill (which later would be reimbursed) and said she'd be waiting for them whenever they arrived.

Jeff was so beat, he slept in his car and left Cane overnight with the vet for observation. Next day, the pair left. When they arrived at Jeff's aunt's home, Cane was coming around beautifully. It had been a close call, yet Jeff felt someone, somewhere, was watching over them.

They arrived at his Mom's place – a healthy dog and a famished owner! Cathy was so pleased that her sister had been there to help Jeff when he needed help.

For the next two years, Jeff worked in Alberta and loved it. He also rebuilt his relationship with his Mom. She'd always lived so far away from him that they'd never spent much time together.

She was happy to have her son during her period of mourning. He was such a big help in so many ways. They became close again and Jeff thoroughly enjoyed this time with Cathy.

Meanwhile, back in Niagara, Cathy's Mom (Jeff's Nana) found out she had cancer. For a while, Cathy flew back and forth between Medicine Hat and Niagara, but she finally decided to sell her house and move back to take care of her.

It just so happened that Jeff had been laid off, so the two of them returned to look after Nana.

Once again, Jeff's timing was perfect. He and Cathy moved in with Nana, who owned two houses side by side. They needed a lot of work. Jeff's new job! He remodeled Nana's house and became her primary caregiver.

Then, she suffered a stroke and was confined to her bed or wheelchair. Jeff built ramps in the house. There was no way he'd put his Nana into a nursing home.

For the next two years, Jeff and Cathy took turns caring for Nana. Her cancer was in remission.

Jeff would come in for a haircut and tell me how he was so tired – Nana had been up eight times the night before and he was changing diapers, making her comfortable. Not too many young men would do that for their grandmother.

I would sometimes tell him, "It's time you met someone. Why don't you try a dating service?"

He just looked at me and said, "Think about it. I go out on a date and she asks me where I live. So I say with my mother. Then she wants to know where I work and I say I take care of my Nana and change her dirty diapers.

"She'd say, 'Don't you have a job?' and I'd tell her I haven't worked in two years. How is that going to sound to some girl I'm on a date with?!!"

From the Hairdresser's Chair

I chuckled. "You're right, Jeff. But some girls would just see you as a very compassionate person.

He said, "No thanks. I'll just wait until I have a new career up and running and I have my own house."

The 24-hour caregiving was taking its toll on Jeff and Cathy. They knew Nana's days were numbered and Jeff wanted to figure out what kind of career he wanted. Something where he could bring Cane along.

Driving a transport truck had always appealed to him, but the course was $10,000. He'd been working for the past two years looking after Nana, but not for a pay cheque. There were no funds saved for him to go to school.

Nana's mind was still sharp. She helped him figure out financing and helped him with the deposit. Once again, the timing was right for Jeff. He and Cathy were able to put Nana in a daycare a few days a week, allowing him some time for school and giving his Mom a break.

He started his 6-week course and loved it, passing all the exams with high 90s! This career was meant for him!

Jeff completed his course and was offered a terrific job immediately. He came home to tell Nana he got a great job with a reputable company and he would be starting work next week. She was thrilled for him. He tucked her in, gave her a kiss and she drifted off to sleep.

She passed away that very night.

Perfect timing yet again. Jeff and Cathy were at peace with themselves. They'd done all they could for Nana for the past two and a half years. Nana was ready to let go and they were both so glad to have been there for her.

Jeff's a kind man with an easy-going nature. His love and compassion for his Mom during the death of her husband and for his Nana during her last years have brought him to a place of fulfilment, gratitude and joy.

He's on the road now, with his own transport truck and Cane still beside him, loving every minute.

Life Lesson from the Chair: *Karma. Synchronicity. The kindnesses we offer others are always returned to us. Perhaps not right away, but when we need them most.*

Until next haircut…

From the Hairdresser's Chair

Addy's Friends Give Her the Best Lift Ever

My clients, Tom and his late wife, Ellie, had a disabled granddaughter named Addy. If you recall, I told you about her in an earlier story.

Several birth defects had left her confined to a wheelchair for the rest of her life. She eats through a feeding tube. Her parents, Kerrie and Chris, have to lift her to carry her from one place to the next.

Although her body is lean and long, Addy has no muscle mass or control; she's a dead weight to lift. The older she gets, the heavier she grows.

Her weight was becoming too much for her parents and caregivers to handle so Kerrie and Chris decided to get a wheelchair lift for their van. But it was going to cost $15,000 they didn't have.

Although the government had provided many grants to assist them with Addy's care and survival, they would not agree to pay for the lift.

In order to be funded, Kerrie would have to quit her job; that wasn't going to happen. They said Kerrie and Chris "made too much money".

What does that mean? Yes, they lived comfortably in a modest home, but they'd already spent thousands of their own money to make Addy's life the best they possibly could.

Both would take time off work for her many appointments. They remodeled their home to make it accessible to her.

They were resigned to taking out a loan to pay for the lift when Addy's Aunt Kathy came to the rescue, suggesting they have a fundraiser.

Kathy works in the Emergency Department of the healthcare system where she and her colleagues have formed a closely knit group. Everyone knew Addy's story and wanted to help.

They were sure they could raise at least half the amount needed to buy that hydraulic lift for Addy.

This amazing team of professionals pulled together and formed a committee to organize and advertise the fundraiser. It was a lot of work for a lot of people, but they were overwhelmed at the level of support they received.

People generously donated money, gifts for draw prizes – even food for the buffet the night of the fundraising event. Tickets were selling like hotcakes!

More than 200 people came to Addy's fundraiser! When the evening ended, the organizers were exhausted, but they – and Addy's family – were overjoyed at the response.

From the Hairdresser's Chair

Next day, they were surprised to find they'd beaten their goal. Kerrie got a phone call that $17,000 had been raised for Addy's new ride! She was overwhelmed and so very grateful for the support her daughter received.

Today, everyone's life is easier thanks to the new chair lift for Addy, who gets to enjoy the world a little more.

Life Lesson from the Chair: *Human beings are hardwired to help each other. But people will never know you need their help unless you ask them.*

Until next haircut…

Big Mike to the Rescue

Jan likes early evening hair appointments so she can go home after work, have a coffee and then travel the twenty minutes it takes her to get to my salon.

About ten minutes before her appointment, Jan phoned me. All I heard before she was cut off was, "I have a flat tire!"

Calling back, all I got before the phone died was "I'm on the highway." I was almost finished another client's hair and explained that this wasn't sounding very good. My client said, "Just do what you need to do."

I pulled out Jan's card. Luckily, I had her daughter's phone number. When I called, she said she'd heard from her Mom but had been cut off, too. She had no idea where she was, either.

"I know she's on the highway. But where?"

The long stretch of highway between Jan's home and my place is very dark, with no streetlights. I tried calling again. This time, I asked her right away, "What exit are you near?" I thought she said "Mountain" before the phone died yet again.

I called Jan's daughter back and told her that her Mom was near Mountain Road. For some reason, I was getting through for about three seconds, yet Jan's daughter had no phone connection at all.

She asked me to phone her Mom again and tell her that Big Mike was on his way to help her. I called, relayed the message about Big Mike and the phone went dead again!

"Well, at least we know she'll be okay," I thought, going back to finish my client's haircut. I knew Jan wouldn't be making her appointment tonight. It would be too late by the time she got settled.

Shortly after, I got a phone call from Jan's daughter. She was with her Mom on the highway and Big Mike was busy changing her tire.

Finally, I just had to ask. "Who is Big Mike?"

"He's our handyman. At least, that's how things started. We hired him to help with things around the house, but now he's more like part of our family. We have him over for dinner a lot because he has no family of his own in this area.

"He rescues us all the time from broken water pipes to cleaning the eaves trough. My kids just love him and he's always there for us. Everyone should have a Big Mike!"

Jan was so happy that Big Mike had rescued her on the highway. It was good, too, that we had enough phone connection to locate her. Gee – what did we ever do thirty years ago without cell phones?

Life Lesson from the Chair: If you can't have a Big Mike in your own life, perhaps you can be one in somebody else's.

Until next haircut…

Gerry Just Does It

In 1954, Gerry was born in Toronto, Ontario, to an Italian immigrant family. At birth, she was born with a disability that resulted in her having but one arm, and two fingers on her only arm. Many thought she was a thalidomide baby, but her mother hadn't taken any drugs for morning sickness.

It was common in those days for parents to send their children with a disability to an institution. The doctors weren't even sure how long little Gerry would live. Gerry's parents accepted her disability and when asked if they wished to do that, said, "Absolutely not!"

Gerry wouldn't find out what had happened in her mother's womb until 2011.

It was her allergy doctor and pediatrician who first suggested that Gerry research Amniotic Band Syndrome. Although the chances are about 5000:1, ABS happens when fibres wrap around the fetus' limbs in the amniotic sac. Pulling taut like strings, they restrict blood flow and impede proper development.

By age five, Gerry had been fitted for her first prosthesis – a standard hook with an elastic band that was very difficult to use and required great upper body strength. She was very petite, but she managed.

From the Hairdresser's Chair

When she was 10 years old, the Crippled Children Centre were experimenting with a myo-electric hook. It had pushbuttons and the user had to carry a battery pack, an amplifier, and deal with wires and plugs everywhere. Gerry was the first person in North America to test out this electric hook.

Unfortunately, it broke down daily. The technology offered many new opportunities to do things. It was a lot of responsibility to have to deal with. The battery pack had to be charged every night. The loose wires and plugs had to be handled carefully. When the equipment broke down, Gerry would be picked up from school by cab and taken to the Crippled Children Centre for repair work. She would be calling the prosthetist regarding the breakdown of equipment; taxi pick-up; and arrange to have school work and assignments.

During the 1960s, Gerry went to a segregated school for children with disabilities.

Gerry understood what it felt like to be helpless. When Gerry was a youth, a team of doctors observed her in her underwear during a conference. She felt so exposed and vulnerable, once again like the guinea pig she'd been when given the prototype hook. Although she always felt like a piece of someone's research, Gerry was nevertheless grateful to the doctors for trying to help her.

In Grade 9, Gerry attended a regular high school. She was very shy and felt uncomfortable there. Although she did make a few good friends, her shyness kept her from getting involved at the school. Upon graduation, she went off to university to get her degree in Social Work. With all she had been through, Gerry made a promise to herself, that she would be a counsellor of some sort, to help another person going through personal struggles to follow their dreams.

It took a few years for Gerry to get the job she desired. Her first job was sorting used clothing. She did a lot of volunteer work in order to gain the skills and experience she needed for that dream job. She was petite and people always underestimated what she could do!

Finally, she was hired as a social worker. She continued to volunteer and landed her ideal job as a counsellor in the social service industry. She stayed very determined and kept her eye on what she wanted. In time, it was hers – her ideal job!

Gerry had met her future husband in university. They married and had two beautiful little boys. Gerry needed no extra help in raising them. She learned at a very young age to just get on with things and figure out a way. While raising her young family, Gerry went back to school to earn her Master's degree.

Someone once surprised Gerry by asking, "What does it feel like to have only one arm?" She said, "I don't know! What does it feel like not to have a million dollars?" What a great answer, from the ever-feisty Gerry!

From the Hairdresser's Chair

When you first meet Gerry, you see a beautiful smile and twinkling, dark eyes with a spark of mischief. Her positive attitude spills over on you and her soft giggles make you smile. She has a wonderful way of communicating that makes you feel at peace in her company.

Gerry now enjoys her retirement and has found a new purpose in helping others achieve their dreams. Her company, *Untapped Potential*, is growing and she enjoys coaching and mentoring her clients.

Today's technology opens up so much potential and opportunity for those with disabilities. Gerry shows her clients how to follow their dreams and go wherever their passion leads. As her mother (and Nike) would say, "Just DO it!"

Gerry loves public speaking. Her greatest joy remains her family; husband, boys and soon, a grandchild. And did I mention her four dogs? Gerry has always lived life to the fullest and encouraged those around her to do the same.

I've enjoyed having Gerry in my chair. Her determination in overcoming obstacles few of us can imagine and her selfless giving to others inspire and empower me.

Life Lesson from the Chair: *There's an answer to every question, a solution to every problem and a way around, over, or through every obstacle we face. Smarts alone are not enough. We need the grit, too.*

Until next haircut...

Betty's "Family Tree"

Betty became a client of mine just after her husband, Len, had passed away of cancer. She was young and vibrant, with two young sons in their early teens.

Len was buried in a beautiful spot with a huge tree nearby. Whenever Betty visited his grave, she would gaze at that tree and think that, someday, she'd like to sit under it and read a book. It was so pretty and peaceful.

Betty's young boys were now being raised without their Dad. Betty had kept the farm where they lived and did a fine job of raising them on her own. The boys helped out a lot. Betty had learned how to operate the tractor. She even made minor repairs and became very good at fixing many things on the farm.

She also kept her boys involved with church. The whole family had a strong faith that helped them heal their loss.

A number of years later, when the boys were ready for college, Betty married Marty. But, she could never bring herself to sell the black Corvette that had been Len's joy.

It was stored in the barn nearby. Whenever Betty took it out for a spin, she could feel Len's presence and fond memories came flooding back.

From the Hairdresser's Chair

When Betty's older son, Skylar, got engaged, she and Marty were pleased to host the wedding at the farm and were busy getting the property ready for the big event. It was a perfect day, and again, Betty felt Len's presence during the ceremony. It was beautiful.

Not long ago, Betty came in to get her hair done and told me, "I have a God story to share with you!" She had ordered a book called *Killing Lions*.

"I thought it would be a good read for my sons because it's about a conversation a father had with his son. Since their Dad was gone, I thought they'd enjoy the book."

She continued. "On the 15-year anniversary of Len's death, my younger son, Travis, called and suggested that we go to his Dad's grave together. Usually, I'd go visit alone, but I was happy to have him tag along."

When Travis arrived, he said, "Let's take the Corvette!" She smiled and said, "Sure!"

Just as they were about to leave, Betty looked in her mailbox. There was the book she had ordered for her son.

"What a coincidence," she thought, slipping it into her purse. Off they drove in the Corvette.

They went to Len's gravesite and spent some time there. Travis noticed that beautiful tree and suggested that they sit under it for a while. Betty smiled again as she remembered how often over the years she had pictured herself sitting under that same tree, reading.

She opened her purse and pulled out the book. She gave it to Travis and he read the subtitle: *Conversations from a Father with his Son.*

As Travis started reading, Betty was filled with joy to think of all the lovely gifts from God that had come to her that day.

Life Lesson from the Chair: *Nothing is a surprise to God. What we call coincidence has been carefully planned in advance for our ultimate good. That doesn't mean we don't have free will; we do. It's just that God knows exactly what choices we'll make.*

Until next haircut…

Susan Senses What Others Can't

Susan was a client of mine. Now she lives in Chicago, so I only see here once a year. We keep in touch by phone and texting. Ever since childhood, Susan has been able to connect to the other side as an intuitive. Over the past 20 years, she has connected hundreds of people to loved ones who have crossed over.

It all started when a friend asked Susan to connect her to a loved one. She casually gave it a try and discovered that she immediately received visual pictures in her mind (clairvoyance). She could also hear (clairaudience) and had a sense of the subject's personality and feelings (clairsentience).

Then another friend requested a reading. Until that point, she had only connected to her own departed family members and to her personal spirit guides and angels.

More and more opportunities presented themselves for her to make connections to spirits and their loved ones here on the Earth plane.

In 2012, Susan had an opportunity to study with a globally celebrated spiritual teacher and six sensory consultant named Sonia Choquette. After studying with her for a year, a new "knowing" was awakened in Susan (claircognition). She'd always felt it, but now it was different, stronger.

During a meditation, she was given a direction: "It's time". Time for what? Time to be of service to a greater audience. So Susan began intuitive medium readings on a regular basis.

When she gave me a reading over the phone, I was amazed at its accuracy. It was full of precise information that allowed me to help my cousin Betsy with my Aunt Rose. (I've changed their names here).

Aunt Rose had suffered with Alzheimer's for 10 years and had been failing for quite some time. She didn't know anyone except her daughters and son who visited regularly. Her daughter, Betsy, worked down the hall and would see her a few times every day. They were very close.

Poor Aunt Rose's body slumped in her chair. It was getting hard for her to keep her head up. Her muscle mass was deteriorating slowly. It was so sad to see her slipping away, mentally and physically.

Fortunately, Rose was still eating. Somehow she seemed to know that her family was around and she was deeply loved. Many patients at this stage could still live for quite some time.

Betsy saw her Mom every day, seven days a week, but she was soon to leave for a three-week holiday in Italy. It was hard for her to leave her Mom for that long, however, she knew she could count on her sisters and brother to check on Rose every day she was away.

Before leaving, Betsy gave her mom the longest, biggest hug ever and said, "Mom, this hug has to

From the Hairdresser's Chair

last us three weeks!" Rose seemed fine when Betsy left. She had told her family Rose's wishes in the event that anything happened while Betsy was away. Everyone agreed that she would be cremated and the service wouldn't be held until Betsy's return.

Rose was 81. Anything could happen. Betsy left on her trip feeling confident her Mom would be well taken care of.

Betsy had only been away four days when she got word that Rose had passed away suddenly in the night. It was as if she had needed to be alone to make her exit to the other side.

Betsy was devastated to know she wasn't at her Mom's side when she passed. She kept calling the travel agent, asking for flights home when her husband, Jim, reminded her of the plan.

She knew she had to stay in Italy. Everything was taken care of at home and the funeral would be in three weeks when she returned.

I happened to be on the phone with Susan three days after Aunt Rose passed away and we ended up having an unplanned reading. I asked Susan if it would be too soon to tap into my Aunt Rose's spirit and she offered to try, and see what we'd get.

The information that came through was so accurate, I had to call my cousin in Italy and share it.

243

Susan had relayed to me the message that Rose could no longer stay in that heavy, slumped-over body. She had wanted to exit a year ago, but she knew her family would have a difficult time then. She hung on as long as she could.

Rose now feels free and has this huge smile on her face. I commented that everyone had always talked about her beautiful smile.

I had also asked Susan who was waiting for Rose when she passed over. The list of people shocked me, it was so accurate.

To name a few, she described my grandparents (her parents) to a tee; a small child - Rose's one-year-old granddaughter who had died 20 years before, and of course, her husband, Jay. Susan described him perfectly.

Then she mentioned that Betsy had had a near miss in an automobile accident the day before. It had been a close call in a narrow street, but Rose and two others had been watching over her.

Susan kept saying that Rose was relieved because she just couldn't have taken the disease of her brain and her heavy body any longer. She was free of all the pain and now surrounded by loved ones who she had missed.

I thanked Susan for the reading and thought, "I need to get in touch with my cousin. This reading will give her comfort!"

From the Hairdresser's Chair

I contacted another relative for the number in Italy where I might reach Betsy. I'd written down everything Susan had told me. It gave her so much comfort and peace.

Betsy confirmed the near accident the previous day which served to prove her Mom's spirit had been in touch with her through Susan.

It was a tearful conversation. Betsy felt so blessed to have received this gift. She attended many churches during her trip where she would light candles and felt the presence of her Mom. This allowed her to feel a wonderful closeness to her Mom's energy for the rest of her trip and brought her great comfort.

Susan's gift brings such peace and joy to those of us who experience this wonderful connection to our loved ones.

Life Lesson from the Chair: Whether or not you believe in spirits and connecting with the afterlife, the universe is a mysterious place we can never fully understand. Keep your heart open to possibilities your mind may not be able to comprehend or imagine. Yet.

Until next haircut...

Johnny O

Sheila has such amazing grandchildren! I've never heard of kids being so driven. These two, in particular, are sure to succeed in their adult life.

When Johnny was eight, he started singing. His older sister, Darian, loved making videos and she started filming Johnny with their parents' video camera.

She gave him the music, taught him all the moves and told him what to wear. It all started as playtime for the brother and sister.

Darian became like a second Mom to Johnny and the two performed as one when they worked together, making their videos. After many practices, they decided to upload a video to YouTube. It was called *Johnny O Sings Mistletoe*.

In no time, Johnny became noticed. He's a very charismatic and charming boy, like a young Justin Bieber.

Realizing how serious their kids' filmmaking was becoming, Johnny and Darian's parents enrolled him in singing and acting lessons. For Darian, they purchased better video equipment and editing software.

Johnny's singing improved and Darian had no problem figuring out the new camera and programs.

From the Hairdresser's Chair

The pair's videos attracted a bigger and bigger audience on YouTube. Fan mail started pouring in from all around the world. Johnny received lots of mail as well as hats, underwear and candy!

He and Darian started a small business, selling bracelets, hoodies, t-shirts, hats, pens and even skateboards. Johnny was loving all the attention!

Darian continued to choose the songs and even wrote three original pieces for him to sing. She kept choosing his clothes, shoes, and hats – whatever he was wearing. Johnny just went along, letting his Big Sis dress him. He was having the time of his life!

Before long, Darian was doing video underwater, for special effects. The girls are all over Johnny! Luckily, he has three sisters so he's used to being around females.

In 2012, the family went to Los Angeles on vacation. They took Darian to see a film and recording studio. The studio recommended that Johnny get an agent! He did and has since appeared in TV commercials for Nutella and Cadbury Easter eggs.

He's also been on TV, in shows like Tiny Talent and he has sung the national anthem at hockey games.

Johnny also performed at the Christmas Tree Lighting Ceremony in Oakville, Ontario, and has opened for the MiniPops on Canada AM. Wow! He's only 12!

And Darian is so creative! She came up with an idea to tour Johnny's bedroom. On video, he walks through and talks, then a prize is offered for watching the video. The winner gets a private phone call from Johnny. The young girls on YouTube went wild over this!

Johnny and Darian's "small" business is now earning BIG money. Johnny has over 50,000 Followers on Twitter and most of his songs have had between one and three million views on YouTube.

One of his songs, "Problem", won a YouTube Kids' Choice Award for "Most Meaningful Message". (It's one of the videos that Darian filmed underwater).

Darian is still in high school; of course, she wants to major in film studies. There are some film schools in Canada, but Los Angeles is where she wants to go.

Her parents made a huge decision to move the whole family to LA for a year or so. That way, Darian can obtain dual citizenship like her Dad, who travels back and forth for business. They'll keep their home in Oakville, coming back after a year.

From the Hairdresser's Chair

Darian will probably stay in LA to attend film school.

Their parents deserve a lot of credit. Johnny and Darian's success would not have happened without their support and their Mom driving them all over the place.

The family has been in LA for a while now and they're loving it. I can't wait to hear what happens next!

Life Lesson from the Chair: *You're never too old – or too young – to share your talents and gifts with the world.*

Until next haircut…

Luke's Got the Draft on Tap

My brother, Peter, and his wife, Lisa, moved to Canmore, Alberta 21 years ago where they became the proud parents of three boys: Simon, Luke and Noah.

Our parents had been hockey junkies; Peter was playing hockey from the age of four. So it was only natural that he should start his own boys in hockey at a very early age.

As the only female at home, Lisa finally succumbed to being at the arena in all her rare, spare time. Hockey was her life, too. She loved watching her sons play. My brother, now in his late 40s, continues to play and coach.

All three boys are excellent players, but the middle one, Luke, dreams of playing in the NHL.

My Mom and Dad were thrilled to see all their grandsons play, going out West many times over the years to watch their games and visit the family. Luke would often come to Toronto to play, drawing eager spectators from among his Ontario relatives.

Many years ago, I attended one of his games and couldn't believe how professionally these kids were playing. My brother said it cost over $10,000 a year for him and his three sons to play.

From the Hairdresser's Chair

They had a massive room downstairs that looked – and smelled – like a locker room! There was hockey gear everywhere, plus much-needed hooks, shelves and benches.

Back in the day, my nephews would call me for hair advice. The team all wanted to colour their hair the same! Aunt Karen, can you give us some advice, please?

Whenever they visited Ontario, they all arrived with long hair, waiting for me to cut, colour and do my magic! Whenever I went their way to visit, I always made sure to take along my tools.

Doing the boys' hair gave me some alone time with my nephews. It's not easy having a long-distance family relationship, but this helped me get to know them better.

Luke's star started to rise at the early age of seven. By the time he was eight, he was playing well above his age level with his older brother. Then he was playing spring hockey on an elite team: the Calgary Jr Flames.

All three of the boys travelled to play hockey, which led to the whole family juggling schedules to meet everyone's needs. Luckily, Peter was self-employed and could assist the boys in their hockey life. Mom, Lisa, was very accommodating, too.

Because Luke was smaller than his brother, Simon, he had to work very hard to build his strength up. What he lacked in height, he made up for in bulk.

At age 15, Luke left home to billet with Simon in Airdrie. He was very homesick, but stuck it out. Peter and Lisa took in countless hockey billets over the years, too. Their grocery bills were astronomical trying to feed these hungry, growing boys!

Luke had a goal and nothing was going to stop him. He knew that to play in the NHL, he would have to fast track by playing in the Western Hockey League (WHL) first.

The WHL is a major junior ice hockey league based in Western Canada and the Northwestern United States. It's one of three leagues comprising the Canadian Hockey League (CHL) – the highest level of junior hockey in Canada.

Luke left the Alberta Junior Hockey League in his hometown of Canmore and started playing for the Kootenay Ice WHL team that drafted him in the third round of twelve. By the spring of 2014, Luke had made the NHL draft prospect list. When draft day cam the whole family was patiently waiting and watching. First pick – nothing. Second pick – nothing. Third pick – nothing. The draft passed him by that first year. He was very disappointed.

Still determined, Luke trained hard that summer, both on and off the ice.

In the fall, Luke was invited to play for the Toronto Maple Leafs rookie camp which was

From the Hairdresser's Chair

holding an exhibition tournament in London Ontario. Our family was ecstatic! When the Leafs last won the Stanley Cup in 1967, I can still hear how my Mom and Dad (mostly my Mom) were screaming while we were trying to sleep upstairs.

They were huge Leaf fans, no matter what! Even after my Dad passed away, my Mom continued to support the Leafs. She is now turning 80 and what a joy it was for her to see her grandson, Luke, play with her beloved Toronto Maple Leafs. It was amazing!

This year's NHL draft is in June and Luke is beyond ready! Here is an excerpt from an article written in the Cranbrook Daily Townsman at the end of this season: (His proud Aunt can't resist sharing them!)

> Prior to puck drop Friday, the Kootenay Ice presented team awards for the 2014-15 season. Forward Luke Philp hauled in the most hardware, being recognized for four separate awards, including team MVP and Fan Club Player of the Year.
>
> "He's easily one of the hardest-working guys in this league," said Ice goaltender Wyatt Hoflin. "No matter how his game's going -- sometimes pucks aren't bouncing the way he wants them to -- but he still battles. His work ethic is something that every player should strive to have. It's something you can look up to."
>
> Philp has had a banner season as he led the Kootenay Ice in scoring with 82 points (30G, 52A). His assists total is a new career high as

is his point total, having surpassed his marks from the 2013-14 campaign (46A, 77pts).

"I'm extremely honoured about that," Philp said of his awards of recognition. "To get the Players Award, that's awesome -- it's probably the best feeling you can have, knowing your teammates think about you like that. To get the fan award, too, that's pretty cool. But I couldn't have done it without my teammates. There are a lot of guys who could have also had those awards."

Luke got a phone call just the other day from the Philadelphia Flyers, saying they were interested in drafting him, but nothing is guaranteed.

He recently ranked 120th on the central scouting list and has now moved up to the 105th position.

If no one drafts him this year, Luke will need to make choices about going to school or perhaps playing overseas. Our hope is that Luke did enough this year to open some eyes to his potential and maybe he'll be picked in the draft!

Life Lesson from the Chair: Our failures only defeat us if we let them. Learn from them and leave them in the past, with no regrets. It's what you do today that will create your future.

Until next haircut...

SPECIAL BONUS SECTION:

Debbie Does Hair-dos Too

I have a friend Debbie Ivison, she is also a hair stylist and former owner of Salon Cappelli, in Toronto. When I told Debbie about my book, she was very enthusiastic about the project and sent me some of her own tales from the hairdresser's chair.

Now, please understand that Debbie's perspective on life and her experience are completely different and her stories are quite unlike the ones you've read of mine. Debbie insists that these stories are sad, but I think the way she tells them is quirky and darkly funny. You decide.

In Deb's words...

I had a wedding party booked, to do hair and make-up for the bride and her bridesmaids. Everything went great and off they went.

A few days later, a woman came into my shop. As I worked on her hair, she mentioned that she worked at the place where the wedding reception had been held. I asked her if so-and-so (my client) had gotten married there.

"Oh, yes!" she exclaimed. "Didn't you read in the paper what happened at that wedding?"

My colleagues and I had no idea what she was referring to.

"Well, it seems that the groom decided to have one last fling with the chambermaid in their hotel. He was very forceful; in fact, he raped her."

That marriage didn't last very long. I wonder, "Was it the hairstyle that drove him mad?"

Life Lesson from Debbie's Chair: *We may never know what far-reaching effects our smallest actions may have.*

*****

One of the things I loved most about doing people's hair was talking to my clients about everyday life. We would chit chat, laugh and share all our experiences.

Joanne was a wonderful client. We liked each other a lot and would often hang out together, away from the salon.

One day, she asked me to perm her hair for a photo shoot. She had arranged it in order to create a long-time keepsake.

I happily gave her a perm but I never saw the photograph until a friend of Joanne's called to tell me she had passed away. I was surprised and even more shocked to learn that she had collected samples of sleeping pills from various doctors then quietly committed suicide.

What's really eerie is that she had planned her own "going-away" party. She invited her friends –

including me, her hairdresser – to gather and dine on foods she had chosen for us. There were gifts and games adding to the fun but I couldn't bring myself to stay very long.

As I was leaving, I noticed the picture she had wanted the perm for, as a keepsake.

I admit, her hair did look great!

Life Lesson from Debbie's Chair: You never know how long a person may be in your life, or what troubles her soul. Always be kind.

*****

One cold and dreary day, my husband and I decided to go out for dinner with some friends. It was a great evening, but I was tired and wanted to go straight home.

My hubby decided to go on his own to my salon, where he loves to relax in the aesthetics room. He lies on the bed, plugs in the steamer and unplugs himself with a facial.

As he lay there, quietly relaxing, he heard a very loud noise. The sound of broken glass. No longer feeling relaxed, he got up to investigate and saw a man with a crowbar who had just smashed the window and was getting ready to smash the computer's cash drawer next!

The intruder was as surprised as he was! He made to come near with the crowbar, then thought better of it. He backed off and took off.

My husband phoned me at home to tell the tale. I was sure he was making it all up and didn't believe him! Then I heard the police in the background and an officer came on the line to tell me it was true. It was really scary.

Maybe it was a client who didn't like his haircut and just wanted his money back?

Life Lesson from Debbie's Chair: No matter how bad things may appear, always look for the good in people. And learn to have more trust in your hubby!

*****

A woman once came into my salon with her frail, elderly mother who was there for her usual roller set. Once the rollers were in place, I led her over to the other room where she would need to sit under the dryer. There was a small step to go down and boy! Did she go down!

The poor woman fell hard. And, unfortunately, she passed away.

Guess I should have used the curling iron…

Life Lesson from Debbie's Chair: Even the smallest choices can have unexpectedly big consequences.

Share with us!

Debbie's contributions to this book have been an inspiration for my next book. There are thousands of hairdressers like you, making the world a more beautiful place and helping women feel more confident in themselves.

Before they learned to write, human beings communicated through stories. Some have been passed down through generations. What do children say every night at bedtime? "Tell me a story!" We're biologically hardwired to love a good story.

We all have a story to tell. I'd love to hear YOURS and I know others would, too. If you'd like to share your real-life stories from the hairdresser's chair in my next edition, please...

EMAIL them to me at: hairdresserschair@gmail.com
Or UPLOAD to my website:
www.FromTheHairdressersChair.com

I will personally review all submissions. If yours is chosen, it will be professionally edited. You'll have a chance to review the edited version before publication and will be asked to sign an official release.

In addition to the chance of sharing your stories with a larger audience, you'll also get free publicity for your salon. I'll include a brief bio or story about you and mention your salon's name, location and/or its website.

Your life has changed someone else's, in ways you may never realize. And your stories can entertain, inform and educate so many others if you share them. So go ahead. Tell me a story! YOUR story. I can't wait to read it!

PS – ALL feedback is welcome. I'd love to hear which stories you liked best, learned something from or receive any other comments you'd care to make. Email them to the address above or post them on my Facebook page. Thank you very much!

ABOUT THE AUTHOR

Karen Stocker is a professional speaker, workshop facilitator, and author. She has over 40 years of experience in the salon and spa industry, and specializes in helping Salon owners and their staff to attract and retain the kind of business and clients they really want.

Her company, *Law of Attraction Canada*, is based out of St. Catharines. In her workshops she offers tools, strategies, encouragement and inspiration to move attendees to the next level, personally and professionally, by understanding and applying the principles of this universal law: the Law of Attraction.

She is also a speaker and facilitator with Triangle Seminars based out of Mississauga, and a member of Toastmasters International.

Karen is passionate about helping people and would be happy to customize a special workshop or keynote for your group.

Karen Stocker
Professional Speaker, Law of Attraction Facilitator, Speaker for Triangle Seminars

www.FromTheHairdressersChair.com
www.triangleseminars.com
loacanada@cogeco.ca

/